TEEN

to

CEO

A Journey of
Pain, Purpose, and
Neurodivergent
Advocacy

Kimberley Ashwin

Cover image by: Yesna99, 99designs.com
Book design by: SWATT Books Ltd

First Printing, 2025

ISBN: 978-1-9192119-0-9 (Paperback)
ISBN: 978-1-9192119-2-3 (Hardback)
ISBN: 978-1-9192119-1-6 (eBook)

Kimberley Ashwin
Oxfordshire, OX14 1JU

- Crisis Text Line connects you with a trained crisis counsellor via text: Text: HELLO to 741741.

- While the EU does not have a single unified crisis line, many countries offer national services. However, here are some key EU-wide and international resources:

- Mental Health Europe (MHE) offers resources and links to national helplines across EU countries. Website: mentalhealtheurope.org.

- WHO Europe Mental Health Support provides guidance and links to national services and emergency contacts. Website: who.int/europe.

Contents

Kimberley Ashwin

Chapter 1
Teen Mum

"*Y*our GP forgot to tell us you were pregnant."

The young radiographer's words rang in my ears as she carried out a routine kidney scan.

The look on my face must have been quite something, as she went grey and couldn't stop apologising. The first thing I remember saying, apart from "Don't worry, it's OK," many times over, was, "Don't tell my dad," who was sitting patiently in the waiting room. She nodded and smiled.

She turned the screen around to show me, and that's when I saw him – my boy – for the first time. She estimated how far along I was. I was nearly five months pregnant.

I was 16.

I'd gone to the GP to explore contraception. He carried out a health check and my blood pressure had been high. I'd also been losing weight. I thought I was just shifting my teen puppy fat, which I had attributed to hormones, working, and studying all at once. The scan was precautionary and I didn't think anything of it. Yes, I'd had sex. But we'd used protection.

The drive home with Dad was quiet. I was sick in the car. I'd never been car sick before those last few months and then it all began to make sense. I just hadn't realised. Why should I have done?

My first job, before telling my dad, was to tell the kid's biological father. He wasn't ready to be a dad. We were too young, and I got that.

I plucked up the courage to tell my dad a week later. He wasn't happy. Understandably. He was carrying a lot of trauma. My sister was a teen mum and she'd had her child taken from her.

"That's it. You're going down the same road as your sister. Did you not use anything?" he berated me. I confirmed we had.

"Well, did he put it on his foot?" he snapped.

I tried not to laugh in the moment.

"You've wrecked your life." The shock and disbelief in his voice was palpable.

This moment – being 16 and pregnant – changed everything.

It defined who I was going to become, what was going to happen, and gave me a fierce drive to do better.

I didn't want my child growing up ashamed that his mum was on benefits.

I've always had this innate stubbornness. If someone says I can't do something, I say, "Watch me."

Nature and Nurture

To get a sense of where I've come from, my journey to 16 was far from far from idyllic. My early life was filled with adversity and challenges that shaped me into the person I am today.

Growing up in a family of five, with my mum, dad, older half-sister, brother, and then little old me, we had a lovely home, a dog, and two cats. From the outside, life looked good, but things are never what they appear.

My christening

From the age of three I remember my mum drinking "black tea", which was actually vodka and coke. Strange men would come around and she would disappear for a while, leaving me to draw or colour in front of the TV.

Arguments between my mum and dad could last for hours, with things downstairs being smashed up and dinner time long passing. Although I remember being happy about having biscuits for dinner, this excitement became short-lived when it occurred regularly.

We moved house when I was seven, and things became worse. Violence crept into the home, and I have a vivid memory of coming home from playing with friends to find blood all over the cream carpet. My mum had thrown an ashtray at my father's head, requiring him to have stitches.

She would spend hours in bed crying due to the arguments, and I would lie next to her. Initially it was to try and comfort her, and later this became a safety plan. She would self-harm in front of us regularly, overdosing or cutting her wrists, and would then blame these acts on me, my siblings, or my dad.

Dad started to work more, which meant we had to face much more time alone with our mum. I was lucky, as my sister and brother sheltered me, but as they got older and then my sister left home, this was harder for them to do.

Kim, Mark and Char

I was propelled into experiences no child should have to endure. We would be ridiculed, shamed, and tormented with food and violence. My brother and I quickly learned that she would target whoever was home from school first, so we took turns, giving the other child respite – although my brother took more than his fair share to protect me.

Our dad left several times and then came back. When I was nine years old, he left to live with my grandparents, and things ramped up. One night was particularly bad. It was my brother's turn to deal with our mum, as it was my night off from the abuse. I was fast asleep, when I was shaken awake by my brother. "It's time to go, we're going. We gotta go," he said to me.

In my sleepy state, I got up. Mum sent us in a taxi across town with the purpose of finding out why we weren't invited to our grandad's birthday meal at a pub ten miles away. I found out later that she'd kept ringing the pub repeatedly, ranting, and then getting my brother to do this, and eventually they stopped answering. Off we toddled with a cheque to pay the taxi driver. Why she thought we'd come back, I don't know!

I don't remember the drive much except for it being very dark and quiet, but I do recall walking into the pub, and everyone looking shocked when they turned around to see us both, tired, dishevelled, and hungry. Dad leapt up, came over, and gave us a big hug. My nan and grandad were not far behind, upset and asking what was going on.

Grandad paid the taxi driver, ripped up the cheque in disgust, and walked us back to their house. My dad took us home (my grandparents' house) and put *Cheers* on the telly, and made us a sandwich – this was the best sandwich I had ever tasted – with a packet of ready salted crisps. I was so hungry, I can remember it today as if it were in front of me.

Kim aged 8

Over the noise of the telly, I could hear my dad arguing with my mum on the phone saying we'd never come back, and we were relieved we'd finally get some sleep. We were safe.

The next day, I woke to clean uniforms and a packed lunch, something that had become a rarity with mum. As my grandad took us to school, we sped down the hill, passing yellow fields of rape, their sweet, luscious smell drifting through the car. He smiled at me and said, "You will be OK, darling."

After dropping us off at school and explaining what had happened, I felt relaxed and content until halfway through the day. Then there was a knock on the classroom door, and my heart sank. My mum stood there, stating there was a family emergency, demanding that I leave with her immediately.

I was so scared, but I got up and walked over, hoping the teacher would pick up on my frantic look, read my mind, and stop this from unfolding. She was crying as we walked to the car, saying it was our fault for not returning home. My brother was already in the car and gave me a reassuring half-smile.

We went home, and the violence and craziness started. She locked and barricaded the front door, turned on the oven and threatened to blow up the house with the gas. Our dad was banging on the door at this point with social services in tow. The rest was a blur, and finally we arrived back at my grandparents, with two carrier bags of clothes and our bikes. My nan greeted me with a hug. She made sure we had food and a drink, and began to get our rooms ready for our stay. We didn't live with them for long, but it was the best time in my childhood. I had never felt so safe, loved, and nurtured.

During that time, we met with my mum with my dad, often going for walks with our dogs. They seemed happy; Mum seemed sober. After a few months, they reconciled, and told us that they were going to make a go of it again, that it would be different this time and not like it was before. They thought we would be happy. But we were far from it. We knew what this meant. Life was going back to how it was before.

The first few days back were nice. Mum cooked our favourite foods and acted like a mum. But it wasn't long before the drinking increased, and the abuse started again. It wasn't like it was before. It was much, much worse.

Missed Opportunities

Looking back, there were plenty of missed opportunities to stop what was happening. After we returned to Mum's from our grandparents, I was called to the headmaster's office. There was a man sitting at the desk who introduced himself as being from social services. He asked how things were at home, and I replied simply with, "They are OK."

We had been told by our mum that if we ever said anything, we would go into care, and she would share horror stories about what that would be like. I also did not want to leave my dad. I loved my dad, and I worried about him. If I could tell little Kim now that it was OK to be brave and to say something, I really would.

Another opportunity arose when my sister ran away from home and asked to be put into foster care. Social services came to our home. With my mum in the room next door, I realised if I backed up my sister, they might take me, but then again I might be left to face the repercussions for "telling". So, I said everything was fine again.

The police visited our home multiple times. Mum would call them to say Dad had hurt her, despite him being at work and not at home. One of the most harrowing incidents was when she made us watch her break her fingers with a hammer and then called the police to tell them it was my dad.

The police officer wanted to take her to a refuge, but she would not go without me. I did not want to go, and the police officer enforced the message my mum had been giving – that it was all my fault, which was not helpful. The police left to arrest my dad for something he hadn't done. My brother frantically cycled over to try and tip him off but did not arrive in time. This led to me wanting to become a police officer – someone that would see, and I mean really see, and would help that scared little girl, who was being asked to make adult decisions in that moment. I never did become a police officer, as life had a different plan, but my drive to help others in disadvantaged positions has stayed with me from that moment.

The next day, we drove to the hospital, my mum forcing me to change gear for her as she was in so much pain (I was ten years old), and I had to listen to her telling the health professionals that my dad had done this. I could have said differently, but I did not – I was scared and I felt I had let my dad down in that moment. The fear of what might happen if I spoke up was also overwhelming. I felt trapped in a cycle of silence and complicity, unable to break free.

There were countless other moments when intervention could have changed the course of our lives. Teachers, neighbours, and family friends often saw the signs but either did not know how to help or chose to look the other way. Each missed opportunity reinforced the sense of isolation and helplessness we felt.

Just before I turned 11 my dad left one last time. He had met someone else and there was a shift. He seemed distant from family life, but seemed happy. While my mum dived deeper into her hole of despair – she overdosed and needed hospital admissions – everyone else was tired and unsure what to do.

On 2 February 2000 my dad finally came and rescued us. We went to live with him and my new stepmum. We felt safe – this feeling was something I had not realised was absent until now. We could sleep OK and I still had my dad and my brother – I was OK. We also now had the influence of my step mum – someone who could help to keep us safe and providing stability. We had a second chance of being a 'normal family' (whatever normal is).

As I grew older, I began to understand the complexities of our situation. The fear of being taken away from my dad, the manipulation and threats from my mum, and the lack of effective intervention all contributed to the continuation of our suffering. I truly believe my dad had been stuck in a place where he thought he was doing the right thing – he had no idea she targeted us, or what was going on when he was not there... as he had to work ridiculous hours to just keep a roof of our heads due to mum's chaotic behaviour – I am sure he thought we were safe and things were OK. It was not just about the physical abuse though; it was the emotional and psychological toll that left lasting scars on all of us.

Reflecting on these missed opportunities, I realise how crucial it is for systems and individuals to be vigilant and proactive in addressing signs of abuse. It is not enough to ask if everything is OK; there needs to be a deeper understanding and a willingness to act, even when it is uncomfortable or inconvenient.

But no one joined the dots. No one stepped in. And by the time I was 16, I'd already learned that if I wanted a different life, no one was coming to hand it to me. I'd have to take it for myself.

Not the End of the Story

That chapter of my life could have easily defined me. But I knew I wanted more – for myself, and for the baby I hadn't even met yet.

Before we go further, I want to share why this story matters, and who it's really for.

I have written this book for the "little Kims" of this world – the underdogs. Those that need to be seen and heard, to have someone to back them and recognise their worth. If you've ever felt underestimated, overlooked, or like the odds were stacked against you, this book is for you.

It's not a rags-to-riches story or a polished fairytale. It's about what happens when life knocks you down early, and you decide to get back up anyway. It's about becoming a teenage mum, growing up in chaos, navigating systems that aren't built for you, and refusing to let that be the final word.

I'm now the CEO of a neurodivergence organisation. I work every day challenging stigma and creating space for people who think differently. That work matters to me because I've lived both sides – the struggle and the system.

In the chapters ahead, I'll share how I got here – the setbacks, the small wins, the support I didn't always expect, and the strength I had to grow, one decision at a time. It's a reminder to anyone who's been written off that there's more to come. That the labels people give you don't have to stick. That strength can be built, step by messy step, even when you're scared, tired, or completely unsure of how.

Along the way, I'll also share the lessons I've learned – about resilience, systems, self-worth, leadership, and hope – so you can take what you need for your own journey too.

Whether you're a young mum, someone who grew up in a difficult home, someone navigating their neurodivergence, or someone who's been made to feel less-than, I hope my story helps you see what's possible.

Because your beginning doesn't get to decide your ending. And wherever you are right now, you're not alone.

Kimberley Ashwin

Chapter 2
Not Another Statistic

"I'm not going to be another statistic."

This became a mantra during those early days, especially when no one believed I could do this. But I knew the odds were against me.

Falling pregnant at 16 was far from ideal – and not something I'd recommend to anyone – but it was the moment that snapped me out of the chaos I was slipping into. I could have gone down the same path as my mum or my sister. Instead, I made a quiet promise to myself: *this ends with me*.

I didn't know how I'd do it, or what it would take, but I knew I wanted better for my child. And that meant choosing a different way forward.

The pregnancy wasn't easy. I developed pre-eclampsia and spent much of those months in and out of hospital. At the same time, I was trying to figure out how I'd build a life for the baby growing inside me and how I was going to provide for my son.

My beautiful boy, Ben, arrived four weeks early, weighing 5lb 11oz. I was thrown into motherhood with only a brief idea of what good looked like, from the time I had spent with my nan growing up. I relied on my aunties and uncles to navigate how to parent, even the basics of how to make up a bottle of formula. I felt cocooned by their support and non-judgemental and compassionate education on how to be a good mum.

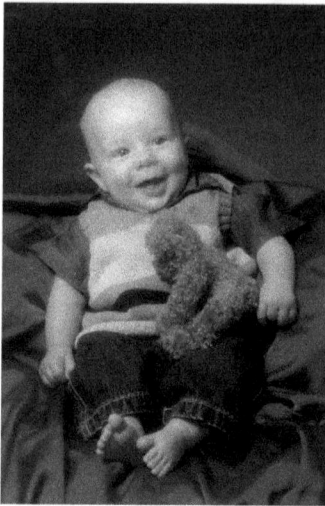

Ben

Life was hard. The sleep deprivation was difficult, as it is for most new parents, but this was unreal, with the challenge of school and work thrown in. While I was never identified as having postnatal depression, reflecting back on it, this is something I can relate to, given my experiences at the time.

I moved out of home, first into a hostel, but before this was agreed, I needed to be screened by social services due to my upbringing and to assess if I was able to bring up my son as I was under 18. It is amazing how strong the maternal instinct can be, and I was adamant to be better and do better for my son. With that, I was all cleared, and we started on our journey.

Research has shown that teenage pregnancy is associated with poorer outcomes for both young parents and their children. Teenage mothers are less likely to finish their education, are more likely to bring up their child alone and in poverty, and have a higher risk of mental health problems than older mothers, but I refused to let these statistics define me. I deserved better, and my son deserved better.

Although they indicate that teenage mothers face significant challenges, success is possible. For instance, those who complete secondary school and go on to post-secondary education are just as likely as older mothers to avoid low-income status. They are more likely to work full time, year round, compared to their adult counterparts. These statistics highlight the importance of education and support in overcoming the obstacles associated with teenage pregnancy.

Teen mothers are also at a higher risk of experiencing mental health issues. They are more likely to suffer from depression, anxiety, and post-traumatic stress disorder (PTSD) compared to older mothers. The stress of balancing motherhood, education, social isolation, and financial responsibilities can take a significant toll on their mental wellbeing. However, with the right support and resources, these challenges can be managed, and positive outcomes can be achieved.

Not surprisingly, financial stability is another significant challenge. Teen mothers are more likely to live in poverty and rely on public assistance compared to older mothers. Approximately 67 per cent of teenage mothers live below the poverty line, and 52 per cent rely on welfare within the first year of their child's birth. These financial challenges can create a cycle of poverty that is difficult to break without access to education, employment opportunities, and support services.

I came across many of these challenges as a teen mum. For one, I lost most of my friends, but there were also plenty of positives. I got to learn with my son and grow together. While many of our firsts together were not within the traditional milestones for a mother and son, there were plenty of these that shaped our lives.

One of the most significant moments was his christening. I organised and paid for it myself, preparing food and managing the arrangements at 17 years old.

Ben's christening with uncle Stephen

I learned to drive for him and passed my test. It cost a lot of money and took a lot of favours for childcare from my nan and grandad, aunts and uncles, and some friends that I had managed to build, but I did it. Unfortunately my dad and stepmum still worked full time and long hours, so had limited availability to help. I borrowed my dad's car for a while, until my parents sold

First car

me their old car, and a friend's husband, who was a mechanic, fixed it up for me. My grandad paid for my first year of insurance to get me up and running, proudly telling me what a milestone this was. I felt like a grown-up and a real mum.

I stayed at sixth form. I gained my A-levels with my son, often with him coming to classes with me. He'd sit in the corner and play when my childcare fell through. My teachers were incredibly supportive. They helped me find a nursery for my son, provided lifts from the hostel to childcare and school, and even bought me pots and pans to start up with.

My teachers suggested I go to university post-sixth form. I laughed initially – someone like me does not go to university – a troubled child, a teen mum. I could hear the years of my mum's voice in my head, telling me I was not good enough. Nonetheless, they believed I could when everyone else wrote me off.

We looked around the local university together, and they helped me with my application for learning disability nursing. I was so nervous at my interview – why would they want a teen mum on the programme? But they saw this as a positive and offered me a place.

In April 2006, I moved into my first home with my son – a council house in a nice cul-de-sac. The housing officer lectured me, stating that these houses do not normally go to *people like me*, but as my previous hostel housing officer spoke so highly of me, this was approved, and I moved in with the help of my nan and grandad. It was time for me to finally grow up. We went on to learn how to cook and manage a home together, and so many more. We were breaking those stigmas and not being a statistic.

Around that time, as things were beginning to feel more stable, I reconnected with Chris – a lad I'd met at school.

We started dating, and he became a brilliant father figure to my son. His family welcomed us both with open arms. His dad and stepmum adored my boy and made a real effort to build a relationship with him. They were kind to me too.

Me & Chris, when we first met

I wasn't used to that. After everything I'd been through, being accepted like that felt unfamiliar but safe – like maybe *this time*, maybe we could build something different.

Learning Point:
You Can Change Your Story

Reflecting on this journey, I realise that becoming a mother at such an early age was the best mistake I ever made. It forced me to grow up, to fight for a better future for myself and my son, and to break the cycle of dysfunction that had plagued my family. It taught me resilience, determination, and the power of love and support.

And for anyone who's ever felt written off – whether you're a teen mum or simply someone facing challenges that feel bigger than you – know this: your circumstances do not define you. Your strength, your choices, and your ability to keep going do.

With determination, support, and a relentless drive to succeed, you can overcome any obstacle and change the path of your story.

Kimberley Ashwin

Chapter 3
Dare to Dream

"*Y*ou are not clever enough to be a community nurse. I suggest you set your expectations lower." That line hit me like a slap. I'd heard worse – but not from my lecturer, someone who was supposed to believe in me.

I didn't say anything at the time, but I'll never forget how small I felt. And how determined I became not to let that be true.

Against the Odds

Starting university in September 2007 was something I never thought would happen to someone like me. I didn't feel clever enough or deserving enough, but I was proud. I was the first in my family to go to university. My brother, who always looked out for me and recognised the importance of this milestone, gifted me a laptop to help with my studies. It meant everything.

But it didn't mean it was easy.

Dropping Ben at nursery for my first day of Uni

I was the only teen mum in the class. I didn't belong. My classmates were out partying, sleeping in, living the kind of life that just wasn't mine. I had a child to raise and a future to build. I felt like an outsider every single day.

I was diagnosed with dyslexia at university, which only made things harder. I struggled in seminars. We'd be asked to read something and then discuss it. I could barely get through a few paragraphs while others had read the whole piece. Their reading speed was insane to me. I panicked. I learned to skim read to keep up, but I felt like I was being left behind as everything took me twice as long.

Chris and I were trying to build a life together. He was doing his mechanic apprenticeship while I juggled lectures, placements, and motherhood. In November 2007, he asked me to marry him. I said yes and set a date straight away – 16 May 2009. He was shocked as I was quick to plan it, but I needed something solid to look forward to, which set off a whirlwind of activity.

Chris and Ben

We dreamed small: me, a nurse; him, a mechanic; a home we could call our own. It doesn't sound like much, but to us, it was everything.

Resilience Required

Then I injured my ankle at the gym. It seemed like nothing at first, but it led to a dystonic[1] episode. My right foot twisted in on itself, and I ended up on crutches with a calliper. Neurology couldn't explain it. The theory was that it was psychological – trauma from my past finally surfacing. It was a stark reminder of how deeply our past can impact our present.

I had to learn to walk again. It was terrifying. It made everything harder – physically, mentally, emotionally. I had to draw on my resilience and determination. I refused to let my health issues define me or hold me back.

However, life had more challenges in store. In September 2008, I discovered I was pregnant again. The news was met with mixed emotions. While there was joy, there was also the anxiety of balancing another pregnancy with my studies. How was I going to do this again?

---

1 Dystonic/ dystonia is a state of abnormal muscle tone resulting in muscular spasm and abnormal posture. The cause is often unknown but can be related to neurological responses to medications, structure changes in the brain and in some circumstances a trauma response.

Connie

Connie was born in May 2009, and the early months of motherhood were hard. Postnatal depression set in, and Chris lost his job. We were skint. Ben, bless him, was the only one who could settle Connie when she cried.

Returning to university in September 2009 was a pivotal moment. Chris had secured another job, and things began to stabilise – kind of. Money was still tight. Sometimes we didn't have fuel to get Ben to school. Sometimes we couldn't afford bread. But we made it work.

Childcare was expensive, and even with help from family, it ate up most of our money. To cope, I dropped some lectures and relied on Moodle[2] to study online. That helped a lot. I found it easier to learn at my own pace, and the parental guilt of missing things eased up, and I could manage my time better.

---

2   Moodle is a free open-source learning platform.

We learned to be resourceful, to prioritise our spending, and we worked out to support each other during the toughest times.

Placements were a game-changer; people often say that you learn more when you start a job and I learned so much more than I ever did in a lecture hall. It was hands-on, practical – exactly the kind of learning that worked for me. I could take in information through doing, through conversation. I helped me to develop my competence and skill set and I started to find my stride.

Emma

Then, in February 2011, I found out I was pregnant with our third child. I was in my final year of uni and the timing was tough. I'd just secured my first nursing job and had to defer it for a year. Emma was born in October 2011, and I got to spend that time with her before finally starting my career in February 2012.

I didn't make it to graduation – I was too pregnant to attend and wouldn't have been able to afford it anyway – but I made it. I qualified as a Learning Disability Nurse. Me. A teen mum. A girl who wasn't supposed to get anywhere.

Graduation

Learning Point:
The Power of Hope

The financial struggles, health challenges, and the journey through university and two more pregnancies tested every part of me. But I learned the power of hope, the importance of dreams, and the strength you get from people who believe in you – and from believing in yourself.

Life doesn't always get easier. But you do get stronger. And that changes everything.

Chapter 4
Proving People Wrong

"Learning Disability Nurses are not considered proper nurses..."

This was a statement I heard a lot during my training, and it was daunting as I stepped into my first job. But it only fuelled my determination to prove my worth and tapped into my drive to prove people wrong.

I'd got this far by refusing to be written off. And I wasn't stopping now.

While I don't agree with people who said this, I do agree it's a completely different field of nursing. It's the smallest branch of nursing but it's incredibly specialist. You're advocating for people with a learning disability – the underdogs. The people who are often at the bottom of society's priorities. We know that people with learning disabilities die prematurely – sometimes up to 26 years earlier – because of health inequalities, and this is not OK.

A typical nurse is trained to assess, treat, and discharge. But in this field, you're making sure nothing gets missed, challenging inequalities, and working through a social model of disability – not a medical one.

My First Job

Given the comment about not being a "proper" nurse, I said, "I'll show you," and landed a job in a community hospital. That first job threw me in at the deep end. There was no easing in or warming up.

They didn't even expect me on my first day. And I'd never worn a uniform before. I didn't know anything about ward nursing and how different it was, but the team were incredibly supportive. Although I wasn't doing clinical care tasks like wound care or IVs, I did find myself learning how to do tube feeds, take bloods, fit catheters, and manage stoma care.

The matron and clinical development nurse really nurtured my confidence. That said, every time I took bloods, I'd get sweaty and clammy, over-relating to the patient and being too cautious. I was learning on the job at full pelt.

Working on the ward was emotionally intense. Many patients were living with dementia, and it took so much patience and empathy while also running and coordinating a busy ward, that was not set up for these needs. As a result, practices occurred that shouldn't have, such as people having restrictive care, and we needed to try and keep them safe. Some days I felt completely drained, helpless, and overwhelmed, questioning whether I was making a difference. Losing patients I'd built bonds with was heart-wrenching, and that grief stayed with me.

I also struggled with the bureaucracy and all the red tape. But I learned how to advocate for my patients and navigate the system effectively. This experience taught me the importance of perseverance and resilience in the face of adversity.

I was offered a promotion, but I soon realised that kind of nursing wasn't for me.

An Important Milestone

The game-changer came when I landed a job as a Community Learning Disability Nurse. I still remember rocking up for that interview. We had to give a presentation on sexual health for people with learning disabilities. I had no budget. Inspired by a programme I had run as a student nurse, I found some creepy dolls on Facebook Marketplace (these looked like Chucky – if you have ever seen the film *Child's Play*, you will get an idea of how creepy they were). I cleaned them up, and used them for a role play about sexual health, consent, and healthy relationships.

I felt so nervous, but this creative and innovative approach impressed the panel, and I was offered the job. It was a moment of validation, proving that courage and creativity could overcome the barriers of self-doubt. Getting the role was a dream come true.

On day one, I was seated next to the band seven lead nurse, who seemed intimidating at first. But I was thrilled, as this meant I got a front-row seat to a wealth of expertise I could learn from. I was a band five nurse in a job I wanted to do, and I felt like I had won the lottery and was set for staying in this role until I retired.

The prospect of collaborating with individuals with complex needs resonated deeply with my desire to make a tangible difference. However, nothing could have prepared me for the emotional and professional demands of the role. I quickly realised that, while the NHS was filled with compassionate and hardworking individuals, the system itself often struggled to provide the necessary resources and flexibility required to truly support neurodivergent individuals.

My initial years were spent specialising in supporting autistic adults and people with a learning disability with severe mental health needs. Many of the individuals I worked with had been through traumatic experiences that had either gone unaddressed or been misunderstood.

One of my earliest milestones in the NHS was working with Jeff, a non-speaking young man repeatedly hospitalised due to self-harm. Standard approaches weren't working and the hospital's chaotic environment only heightened his anxiety and was depriving him of his human rights. It was not his fault. We did not know how to support him. I collaborated closely with his family and the wider team to design a sensory-friendly, structured routine tailored to his needs. As Jeff began to feel safer, his distress reduced noticeably.

Jeff's case opened my eyes to what person-centred care could look like in practice, but it was Sarah's story that showed me the cost to the patient when it's missing. She was in her thirties, withdrawn and mistrustful after years of misdiagnosis. Her autism had been overlooked, her behaviours wrongly labelled as a personality disorder. By advocating for a reassessment, we were finally able to secure the right diagnosis and support. Seeing her begin to articulate her needs – after years of being ignored – was both heartbreaking and affirming. It deepened my resolve to push for better assessments, more training, and a system that sees the person, not just the label.

During this time, I developed a deep appreciation for the power of teamwork. Collaborating with occupational therapists, psychologists, social workers, and families taught me the value of a multidisciplinary approach. Each professional brought a unique perspective, and together, we could create holistic care plans that addressed both the immediate and long-term needs of our clients.

I was well supported by my team, and also by my line manager and team manager. They saw my potential and were not shy in calling this out. They were brilliant – offering advice, listening, just being there. We often faced difficult situations together, and the mutual support and understanding among colleagues created a sense of solidarity and resilience. Knowing that I was not alone in facing these challenges provided immense comfort and strength.

The support extended beyond the workplace. They were genuinely interested in my wellbeing and often checked in on me and my family. Their kindness and empathy created a sense of belonging and made the workplace feel like a second home. This supportive environment was crucial in helping me balance the demands of my nursing career with the responsibilities of being a mother.

But we were still broke. Everyone else would go to Subway for lunch. I couldn't. Childcare was killing us. Both Connie and Emma were in nursery, and we had wrap-around cover for Ben. The fees were £1500 a month, which was more than my entire salary. We could have claimed benefits and been better off, but we weren't going back. But we knew this was short-term pain for long-term gain, and it wouldn't be forever.

Growing Into Leadership

That nurse from my first day, the intimidating band seven, ended up being my biggest champion. She saw my potential early on. I remember her listening to me on a call with a client, and afterwards she just said, loud and clear: "She'll be a team manager one day." I couldn't believe it. That confidence in me stuck.

I loved the work. I progressed quickly, firstly to a band six, and then band seven to cover maternity leave. I supported complex clients, did risk assessments, capacity assessments, the lot.

When the Trust was taken over, I nervously reached out to the new director. We met for tea and carrot cake (which I hate but ate anyway to impress her). She asked me what I wanted to be. I said, "Oh you know, one day I want to be a team manager."

She looked at me. "Really. Is that it? That's a bit boring. Don't you want to be so much more?"

That's when things shifted. She offered me the role of Mental Health Liaison Nurse for autism and learning disability. Together, we carved out a service, despite there being no budget for the role. I ended up developing the reasonable adjustment team locally. We reduced the average length of stay for autistic patients from 400 days to just 12. It became a national exemplar for NHS England.

She became my mentor. She encouraged me to enrol in my first leadership course and introduced me to the world of networking outside my team, on local, regional, and national platforms. She helped refine my rough and ready approach, shaping me into the leader I am today.

Learning Point:

You Don't Need Permission to Succeed

The early years of my NHS career taught me that resilience isn't just about surviving – it's about using every challenge to fuel your growth. From people saying I wasn't a "proper" nurse, to learning on the job, to building a national exemplar service – none of it was easy. But it was worth it.

You don't have to start with privilege to rise. What matters is grit, courage, and the people who see something in you before you see it in yourself.

Whatever your dream is – dare to chase it. And when someone says you can't, just smile and say, "Watch me."

Chapter 5
My "Why"

"*Y*ou are all treated equally but not the same."

This is something I say to my children all the time. They are all beautifully unique and have found it hard to fit in with their peers around them – sometimes feeling isolated, at other times, just finding it hard to keep up.

This statement has influenced my parenting, ensuring each one of them has the mother they need. The one they deserve. The one I never got.

Our Trailblazer

My eldest child Ben is the trailblazer of our household. He has always been talented at sports, and his attitude has also opened a world of innovation and out-of-the-box thinking. Choosing not to follow a traditional post-sixteen education programme, he questions everything. He is fiercely independent in many ways, but also incredibly vulnerable in others, with his big heart and an "I want to help" mentality. Watching him navigate the world has been both enlightening and humbling.

Ben in his MK Dons kit

He is also a naturally talented footballer. He played at MK Dons and RTC Oxfordshire and Buckinghamshire. His sport required massive commitment – time, money, logistics. We didn't have the funds. So, at age nine, when he had the chance to tour with MK Dons in Holland, he raised the money himself. Sweeping drives and helping neighbours with their shopping, he earned every penny. I'll never forget the pride on his face handing over those pound coins to pay for the trip. He was the youngest on the tour and had all the older kids carrying his bags for him. He also earned player of the tournament.

He has also had his own clothing brand, vintage football boot business, and more recently a photography enterprise. Ben now works with us at Autism Oxford UK. He is learning how to navigate the adult world and also how to be a colleague in his parents' business. His natural flair for creativity is showing real promise for marketing and photography, and we have no doubt he has an amazing career ahead of him, wherever his path takes him.

Parenting Neurodivergent Children

Both my girls are neurodivergent – autistic, dyslexic, and with ADHD – and parenting them has taught me more than any degree or job ever could. It's why I care so deeply. Why I fight so hard. Why advocating for the underdog isn't just something I do, it's who I am.

Every family is a blend of personalities, quirks, and traditions, but ours operates on a different wavelength altogether. Our home hums with

creativity, unpredictability, and resilience.
Each of my children brings something unique
to the table. It's their different strengths and
perspectives that keep life both challenging
and rewarding.

This has given me a front-row seat on the unique
challenges and joys of parenting in a world that
often does not accommodate difference. Their
journeys – from thriving in specialist provisions
to the life-changing decision to be unschooled –
have deeply influenced my professional mission
to create services that work for families like ours.

Our eldest daughter Connie was diagnosed
autistic with a pathological demand avoidance
(PDA) profile, which added a whole new
level of complexity to our lives. Autism is a
neurodevelopmental difference characterised by
differences in social interaction, communication,
and repetitive behaviours. PDA is an autistic
profile where individuals have an extreme
avoidance of everyday demands and
expectations due to high anxiety and often have
an overwhelming need for autonomy.

From the outside, she could mask it incredibly
well – charismatic, funny, engaging – but inside,
she was often overwhelmed. As a baby, she
never stopped crying (except for when she
was with Ben). As a toddler, she would explode

with seemingly no warning over things that seemed so minor to us. In primary school, she was emotionally dysregulated most days before and after school, and traditional parenting just didn't work.

Due to her charismatic personality, wicked sense of humour and ultimate ability to camouflage, school never believed what version of our daughter we had to support because of a day filled with the demands and expectations that school placed on her. They did not understand the impact on our family and the impact of their communication and words on my wellbeing and confidence.

She would hold it together all day, then fall apart when she got home. It was exhausting and heartbreaking. They saw the version she presented to them, not the one we had to support after school – the meltdowns, the tears, the hours it took to recover. And because we were young parents, there was an unspoken judgement that we must be the problem.

We had to throw out the parenting rulebook. A PDA-friendly approach felt alien at first, but it was the only thing that worked. We wondered if we were wrong, feeling the breath of school at every move we made, waiting to parent-blame and re-direct emphasis with the loaded question

"Has something happened at home?". This was also layered with the stigma of being a young mum and the perceived perception of us from the wider world. We were still learning what good parenting looked like, let alone parenting a young person with special educational needs (SEN).

This is how I started to develop my specialism around autism and PDA. When we changed our parenting, life changed – she was more settled when we got the hang of this in secondary school, but we needed the world to change for her too, so she could be her best self, which meant she needed to leave mainstream education.

Making the decision to unschool her was the best decision we made. However, for us, life just got even more complicated. People often comment, "I don't know how you do it." To be honest, I don't know either, but what I do know is my family are worth it.

Now in her teens, she is unschooled and pursuing her passion for acro-gymnastics, which has given us so many firsts for her, and we are incredibly proud. She is now embarking on her coaching career.

Unusual Health Conditions

Emma, our youngest, has always had weird and unusual physical health conditions, such as cellulitis on her face as a baby, Henoch-Schönlein purpura (HSP), and shingles as a toddler. She has had intermittent inflammation and pain in her joints, leading to numerous hospital visits, tests, and advocacy. The worry and stress about her health challenges were immense. We constantly questioned if we were doing the right thing for her and if we were making the best decisions for her wellbeing. Despite these challenges, we are incredibly proud of how she has tackled all her health issues with resilience and determination.

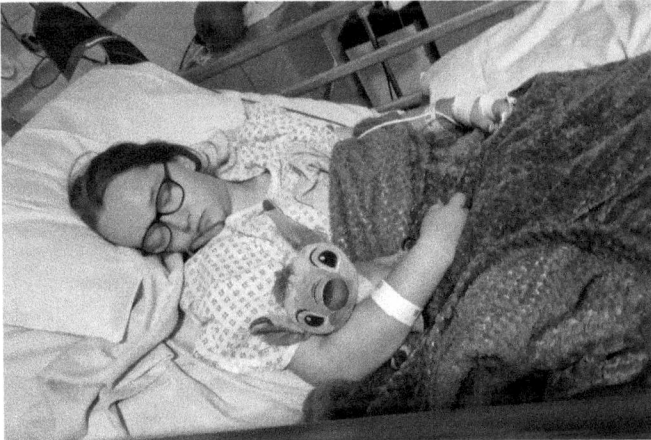

Emma in hospital

She wasn't diagnosed autistic, with ADHD, or specific learning difficulties (SpLD), and retained primitive reflexes until much later, as her older sister took most of our attention. SpLD refers to difficulties in specific areas of learning, such as reading, writing, or maths, despite average or above-average intelligence. Primitive reflexes are automatic movements that are present at birth and typically integrate as the child grows. When these reflexes are retained, they can interfere with motor development and learning.

The guilt that came with this delay was significant. I felt I had let her down – she was always so happy and content, I never felt I needed to worry about her, despite her physical health needs. It was only during the COVID-19 pandemic that we unearthed how behind she was academically and how much support she needed in her own right.

There was yet another fight, starting with the very same primary school that had caused me so much emotional harm when attempting to advocate for my eldest daughter.

A deep breath and off I went again, hitting the same brick walls of resistance in acknowledging any needs or support. We commissioned several reports, Occupational Therapy, Clinical Psychology, Educational Psychology, Speech and Language Therapy and the needs were becoming significant and more complex – yet the school Special Educational Needs Coordinator (SENCO) was still adamant there were no special needs.

We had a defining meeting where I explained that I was still carrying the scars from my eldest's journey within the school. I really wanted to avoid this again and wanted for us to work together. This led to the SENCO getting upset and defensive, but the cold hard truth was that my daughter needed support.

We applied for an Education, Health and Care Plan (EHCP) and were eventually awarded this. We felt secondary school would need to be heavily adapted. She was offered a space at a SEN school, but funding was not available for this until we appealed to the tribunal, and the date was many months after her Year 7 start date.

We were at a crossroads; we needed to work out a way to best support her. We raised funds to privately fund her first term and then set to work on getting the tribunal date brought forward. Finally the local authority conceded and funded the school. This was costly both financially and emotionally. But she was happy. Her confidence was growing and for the first time she was showing competence in her learning and was well supported to be herself.

Our youngest, Emma, has had to live in the shadow of her older siblings. She has had to take a back seat to her older sister, Connie, who often showed jealousy towards her, leading to increased risks for her. We had to spend time mentoring Emma on how to approach her sister and disguise praise for her, ensuring we had discreet but meaningful time for her too. It was hard, as people focused on Connie's sports achievements, yet Emma has so many other accomplishments in her own right. She is the kindest person I have ever met and will always put others first.

Another Challenge to Overcome

Just when we thought we'd been through enough, in 2016, my husband Chris was diagnosed with multiple sclerosis (MS). The same year Connie was diagnosed with autism.

MS is a chronic illness that affects the central nervous system, leading to symptoms such as fatigue, pain, and difficulty with coordination and balance. The progression of the disease can vary, day by day and even hour by hour, but it often leads to significant physical and cognitive challenges.

My husband's first symptom was vision loss. The system bounced him around. The GP said it was an optician issue, and the optician said it was a GP issue. He was finally referred to the eye hospital, and the consultant bluntly said, "You have MS, right?" Like we knew!

It felt like my world was crashing down around me. I was terrified of losing my husband, not just physically but mentally, as the lesions on his brain threatened his personality and character, however his main fear was losing his mobility.

I couldn't fix it, but I could advocate – and I did. I helped navigate the complex health system to ensure he was properly assessed and diagnosed quickly and treatment was in place.

His treatment journey has been challenging. He was prescribed disease-modifying treatments (DMT) to slow the progression of MS and as we sat at the dining-room table together a nurse showed him how to inject himself and explained the horrendous side effects he was likely to endure. For the first DMT he tried, the side effects were often debilitating, causing flu-like symptoms, fatigue, and injection site reactions.

Family

Despite these challenges, Chris has remained determined to manage his condition, and we tried a couple more different ones, before settling on the newest one on the market which he has been on for a few years now. This requires him to go to hospital as a day patient for six-monthly infusions. This wipes him out for a couple of weeks afterwards, and while he recovers, I am a single mum. However, for his determination to support me and his family, I am just in awe of him. Despite the daily pain he experiences and the overwhelming fatigue, he is still very much present for us.

While his newer DMT has slowed the progression of MS, allowing him to adapt, how much and how little he helps depends on how he is feeling. But somehow, we have adapted, just like we always do. We faced it the same way we've faced everything else. Together.

Learning Point:
Know Your "Why"

Our journey has taught us the importance of resilience, adaptability, and the power of a strong support system. By supporting each other, we have been able to overcome significant challenges and build a better future for our family.

Throughout these tough times, the strength of my relationship with my husband has grown, and our ability to collaborate became crucial. We've faced so many challenges – financial, emotional, medical – but we have navigated them as a team. That shared resilience is what holds us together. It powers everything I do.

This is my "why".

Chapter 6
Finding Peace

"Oh well, I have cancer... it is what it is."

My grandad's matter-of-fact comment left me stunned and speechless. He was my idol.

Since having my children, we had visited my grandparents at least twice a week. They always gave us a weekly nanny bag filled with practical items like cleaning products and sweet treats – although you had to be careful if you said you liked something, as it would be in the nanny bag forever more – I'm still getting white buttons 15 years on!

Grief was something I faced during my work, but this was the first time I had to face it personally. What follows are the stories of those losses – and how they shaped my perspective on peace, forgiveness, and what it means to show up when it counts the most.

A Good Death

My grandad had gone to the hospital for test results, which he had massively downplayed. He continued to downplay the severity when sharing the results with others. He had stomach cancer, and he fought it with all his might, undergoing treatment and giving it his best. But after years of fighting, the cancer had spread.

My grandparents asked me to accompany them to his final hospital appointment – I would be another pair of ears, and my nan never liked driving far. We sat in the consultant's room, listening quietly as the consultant explained there were no options left. As we walked back to the car, he simply said "Well, that's that."

Nan & Grandad

My nan brashly told him not to give up hope, but he had made his decision. He'd had enough of fighting and wanted to enjoy the time he had left.

And he did – spending it with his four sons, their wives, and his grandchildren.

Routines stayed in place until they couldn't. When the time came, he passed away peacefully in his sleep, at home, with his wife nearby and one of his daughters-in-law by his side. I believe he knew at that moment that his wife would be OK without him. We would be OK and this allowed him to go. I owed him so much – everything he and my nan did for me growing up – and I used my nursing knowledge to help facilitate this. I wanted to ensure he got the good death he wanted and deserved. It was a privilege.

One of the most profound lessons I learned from my grandad was the importance of embracing the present. Despite the grim prognosis, he chose to focus on the time he had left and make the most of it. This taught me that even in the face of adversity, we can find moments of joy and connection with our loved ones.

Making Peace With Mum

Eighteen months later, I was standing at the school gate when another mum came up to me. "I know your mum," she said. I felt myself go pale, not sure whether to smile, cry, or panic. "Oh, do you?" I replied inquisitively, unsure how she knew the link. She went on to say she'd been cleaning for her and had seen my photo on the wall. She felt she had a duty of care to let me know that my mum was dying.

I hadn't seen my mum since my eldest was born. I made that decision for his safety and mine. I wanted to protect him fiercely from the upbringing I'd had, although it hadn't been easy cutting her out. But despite everything, she was still my mum. Many people can't understand how I can still feel empathy for my abuser, but the reality was she had been a poorly lady for a long time, and that was sad and it had cost her her family.

My mum

I asked what was wrong and was told she had cancer, and only had weeks to live. I managed to hold it together to get home and told my husband at the earliest opportunity. I expressed my desire to see her but also my fear of being hurt. I called my brother. He was blunt and strongly urged me to stay away. He even suggested she might be lying, which was sad but not uncommon for her.

My dad and stepmum were concerned. They worried for my wellbeing and were also dubious about the legitimacy of the information. Emotions ran high as they worried about me getting hurt and everything we had been through, coming back to the surface and jeopardising everything.

But I couldn't let it go. I needed to see for myself. I plucked up the courage to lift the blocks off my social media and messaged her, but I was too late. She had passed away the day before. The only regret I carry in life is missing this moment. I should have trusted my gut. I'll never hesitate like that again.

Her partner was no help, so I organised the funeral and her estate. It felt strange. Hypocritical, even. I had chosen to cut her out. But I couldn't ignore the part of me that needed to make peace. I wrote her a letter and placed it in her coffin. She didn't look like I remembered. She looked peaceful. Less scary.

Chris and I attended her funeral. I sat in the crematorium listening to the eulogy I'd pieced together. It was hard – trying to speak truthfully when the memories were tainted. But I thanked her for the bits she got right. I laid her to rest with her mum, along with some of my anger. It helped.

I realised that even in the most challenging relationships, there can be moments of positivity. Reflecting on the good memories and the lessons learned can help us find the silver lining and appreciate the growth that comes from adversity.

There was a small estate, and I split it three ways. While my brother and sister didn't want anything to do with her affair or the funeral, she was still their mum, and they deserved some sort of compensation. I held back my sister's share. Knowing her lifestyle choices with substances and alcohol, I kept it aside for her funeral.

Saying Goodbye to My Sister

Six years later, that day came. I got a message on Instagram. My sister had been found dead in a hostel. Her son, estranged from her since he was a baby for his own safety, had had the police come and knock on his door, as he was officially her next of kin. The news hit me like a freight train. I wailed. Chris was caught off guard.

My Sister Char and my children

I managed to breathe through my sobs to tell him and he gave me the biggest hug, but it didn't hit the mark. This happened the week before Christmas, as my uncle knocked on the door with presents, and I ran outside and broke down in his arms.

I had to tackle a delicate and complicated non-existent relationship with my nephew and I messaged him, not expecting a reply. But he did. We shared messages. There was a flicker of hope that maybe, out of this, we could build a relationship. But it didn't last. He didn't want to organise the funeral. I understood. His experience of her was different.

But she was still my sister. She protected me once. I owed her a dignified goodbye. So I called the coroner, took over responsibility, and planned her funeral.

The funeral was simple, but I worried it would be a repeat of the lonely service my mum had, however I needn't had worried. Over 30 people came to pay their respects. I read a poem about drugs and how they destroy families. I played a photo tribute to her favourite band, Take That. It was honest. She wasn't a bad person. She had made bad choices. She was a product of the same abuse that I had survived.

Reflecting on my relationship with my sister, I realise how complex and multifaceted it was. Despite the chaos, she had helped shape who I became. And in laying her to rest, I was able to lay down a little more of the pain we both carried.

Learning Point:
The Messy Path to Peace

Grief is complicated. Peace doesn't always arrive neatly packaged. Sometimes you have to make it yourself. I found peace not through forgetting, but through facing it all – the trauma, the contradiction, the mess of love and loss.

Through supporting my grandad, forgiving my mum, and laying my sister to rest, I was able to become more of who I am.

I don't have all the answers. But I've learned that peace isn't always given. Sometimes, we have to claim it. With grace. With grit. And with love.

Chapter 7
Breaking Barriers

"Opportunities don't happen to people like me."

At least, that's what I used to believe. Growing up, I thought public speaking, national recognition, and travelling for work were reserved for a different kind of person. Not for a teen mum from a council estate. But four opportunities shifted that belief entirely, which included my first ever train ride for a speaking engagement, and an invitation to speak at the Houses of Parliament.

It feels important to share these moments now, because they marked a turning point. After navigating the complexity of home life, parenting, and personal grief, these were moments of professional emergence. They didn't just build my career. They helped reshape my sense of self.

My First Train Ride

My first speaking opportunity came from our Learning Disability Consultant Nurse in 2016, who had seen something in me I hadn't yet recognised, and took me under his wing.

He was outward facing and well connected and one day he caught me in the corridor. "Kim, do you want to come and do this talk with me?" he asked, inviting me to co-present on the topic of assistive technology for people with a learning disability. It was at the National Learning Disability Nursing Conference in Manchester.

"You write the slides, you lead it and I'll be your assistant," he said with a grin. I agreed and he said, "Great we'll take the train. I'll meet you on it."

There was just one problem: I'd never been on a train before.

It sounds so simple, doesn't it? But in my late twenties, I'd never bought a ticket and I didn't know how to use a train. It came with a shadow of embarrassment, but this experience taught me that not everyone knows what you think they know and it's OK to learn and grow at your own pace.

To help me to navigate the experience, he patiently met me at the station, and coached me through the whole thing. He literally showed me what to do as if he was teaching someone with a learning disability. The train travel lesson went smoothly, and I soon became a seasoned train user, a skill I later passed on to my children.

First train ride

When we arrived at the event, I remember standing at the front of a full room feeling really nervous. But something clicked. I got through it. I even enjoyed it. And as we walked around afterwards, he introduced me to people at a national level, and those whose publications I'd read. Imposter syndrome was rife that day, but by the end of the trip, I felt a little more grown-up. A little more like I belonged in this world.

The NICE Committee for ADHD Guidance

Shortly after that first train ride, he asked me to go to London for the NICE committee meeting for ADHD guidance in London, as he couldn't go. I remember texting him from the train with "Hey, look at me, being a big girl, going on the train by myself!"

Attending the event was a significant experience. As a contributor to the NICE ADHD implementation group, I helped translate evidence-based guidelines into actionable strategies to improve ADHD care in the UK. My role included offering clinical and personal insights to ensure practical recommendations.

A rewarding part of this work was highlighting families' experiences with ADHD diagnosis and support. By sharing real-world challenges, I ensured the guidelines addressed common gaps and barriers.

These roles deepened my understanding of systemic issues in neurodiverse care, such as long waiting lists, inconsistent service quality, and lack of post-diagnostic support. My contributions aimed to tackle these challenges directly.

Innovation was central to my efforts, whether exploring new care models or advocating for technology integration. Staying updated with neurodiversity research and practice allowed me to propose transformative ideas.

The power of collaboration stood out most. Working with professionals, policymakers, and families highlighted that meaningful change requires joint efforts. Their collective expertise and passion inspire me to strive for better outcomes.

It also reinforced my belief in the importance of lived experience. My personal perspective complements my professional knowledge, enabling advocacy for solutions that truly meet community needs.

The Autism Consultant Nurse Network

Around this time, I came across a Facebook post on a nursing forum where I am a member, which asked if anyone would be interested in joining an Autism Consultant Nurse Network. There was a positive response, and two other consultant nurses expressed interest in helping set it up. The first meeting had a low turnout but was impactful, highlighting the importance of peer support and collaboration among professionals facing similar challenges and sharing values.

Co-chairing the Autism Consultant Nurse Network has been significant in bringing together professionals from across the country to share best practices, address challenges, and advocate for improved care for autistic individuals. Contributions have been made towards shaping national policies and initiatives that impact the lives of those served.

One of the primary focuses of the network is addressing the shortage of trained professionals in autism care. By encouraging collaboration and providing training opportunities, the aim is to build a workforce equipped to meet the diverse needs of the neurodiverse community. Through conferences, workshops, and online forums, a space has been created where knowledge and innovation can thrive.

The network's influence extends beyond the professional sphere. By engaging with policymakers, efforts are made to advocate for systemic changes that prioritise early intervention, holistic care, and accessible services. These advocacy efforts are driven by the collective passion of the members, who are committed to making a tangible difference.

The Houses of Parliament Speech

Both of the roles, co-chair of the Autism Consultant Nurse Network and a contributor to the NICE ADHD implementation group, influenced national discussions on neurodiverse care, and have supported the commitment to systemic change and innovation. They also likely led to a call a little later that I nearly ignored.

I was at a spa with two colleagues when I saw a missed call from the Head of Learning Disability Nursing at NHS England. When I rang back, I found out I was being invited to speak at the Houses of Parliament to celebrate 100 years of learning disability nursing.

Baroness Hollins wanted me there to talk about why I was a Learning Disability Nurse and the impact I'd had. I almost dropped the phone. Me? Speaking in Parliament? I could hardly believe it!

Of course I said yes. I was sent a formal invitation to attend. A very fancy invitation. But then I started to worry. What do you wear to speak at the Houses of Parliament? I was still skint and didn't have anything fancy. But I pulled something together.

I was able to make use of my newly developed train skills, and I remember walking out of the underground and seeing Big Ben, and just being in awe. I felt like I was about six years old, with everything looming large around me. After going through security, I bumped into a colleague I knew, which made me feel more at ease. We got shown into the chambers and a fancy room with fancy food, and I tried to act like I fit in.

As surreal as it was, I delivered my talk, standing tall. It was an amazing opportunity. I felt like I was bossing it!

What These Moments Gave Me

All of these opportunities had a profound impact on my confidence and visibility, and helped me to see myself in a new light. I began to recognise my own strengths and capabilities, which had previously been overshadowed by self-doubt.

The act of preparing for and delivering presentations and talks at such significant events required me to delve deep into my knowledge and experiences, and articulate my thoughts clearly and confidently.

The positive feedback and recognition I received from peers and leaders in my industry further boosted my confidence. Hearing words of encouragement and praise from respected

First Award with Liz and Tim

professionals validated my efforts and reinforced my belief in my abilities. This external validation was crucial in helping me to overcome my imposter syndrome and to see myself as a competent and capable professional.

They allowed me to step out of my comfort zone and embrace new challenges. It elevated my profile and opened doors to further opportunities. I was invited to participate in more conferences, workshops, and panels, which further expanded my network and allowed me to connect with other professionals in my field. These connections were invaluable in providing support, mentorship, and collaboration opportunities, all of which contributed to my continued growth and development.

I was provided with a platform to share my story and insights, which in turn helped to build my professional reputation. As I spoke at these events, I realised that my experiences and perspectives were valuable and that they resonated with others. This realisation was empowering and motivated me to continue sharing my story and advocating for change.

These experiences have also reinforced the importance of continuous learning and development. The feedback and recognition I received motivated me to seek out new learning opportunities and to continuously improve my skills and knowledge. This commitment to lifelong learning has been a driving force in my career and has helped me stay at the forefront of developments in my field.

Good Leadership Makes the Difference

I didn't get here alone. From my early days as a nurse, I had managers and directors who said, "You're going places." They saw something in me I didn't yet see. They nudged me forward. They led with empathy, humility, and a belief in nurturing talent. Their style shaped how I lead today: with curiosity, compassion, and a deep respect for lived experience.

They helped me see beyond my initial aspirations. They encouraged me to think bigger and to envision myself in roles that I had not previously considered. Their mentorship helped me develop the confidence to pursue these new opportunities and to believe in my ability to succeed.

I was propelled into strategic leadership, which I grew to love, and their support and mentorship were invaluable in helping me to navigate this new terrain. I learned the value of empathy and humility in leadership, how to create a culture of trust and collaboration, and motivating others through your actions.

You need to be confident enough to admit mistakes, seek input from others, and prioritise group success over personal ego. When you lead in this way, you build stronger teams, make better decisions, and create a more inclusive environment. Humility involves a genuine openness to others' insights and a willingness to explore and take on new ideas, thinking, knowledge, and behaviours in light of external evidence. It is about making intentional choices to foster growth, respect, and accountability within a team.

As John C. Maxwell, *New York Times* bestselling author, coach and speaker, has said: *"A leader is one who knows the way, goes the way, and shows the way."*[3] The impact of this learning and this knowledge filtered through everything: I became a better communicator, a more visible advocate, and a more confident leader.

---

3   See https://johnmaxwellteam.com/the-power-of-leadership/#:~:text=3)%20Model%20the%20way.,positive%20impact%20in%20your%20world.

Learning Point:
Embrace Opportunities

Opportunities may come unexpectedly, and they may seem daunting, but they are also moments of growth and transformation. By stepping out of your comfort zone and embracing new challenges, you can achieve things you never thought possible. Sometimes, they start with a train ticket and a terrified "yes".

But those yeses build something. And if you let them, they can help you grow into the person you were always meant to be. If you're offered something new – even if it scares you – take the train.

Break barriers and create a path for others to follow. You are capable of achieving great things, no matter where you come from or what challenges you face.

Believe you belong. Because you do.

Chapter 8
Navigating the Storm

"What are we even doing?"

This was a question Chris and I asked each other often in the early months of 2020, knee-deep in work, exhaustion, and sacrifice. We were running on fumes. Then COVID-19 hit, and the world stopped.

Managing the Pandemic

I was still in the NHS at the time, juggling my role as a middle manager with command calls, emergency plans, and parenting our children.

Chris, who was shielding, was being assessed for medical retirement. This added another layer of complexity to our lives. When he did retire, it was a difficult transition for him, as he struggled with the loss of his career and the impact of MS on his daily life. However, it did offer us a lifeline, as there was no way I could continue to work and support our children during the unexpected change on my own.

Our children, already navigating the world differently, struggled in their own unique ways. The lockdown revealed the extent of the educational needs of Emma, my youngest daughter, who had always been a happy and content child but struggled significantly with her schoolwork. As I mentioned earlier, the pandemic unearthed how far behind she was academically, and we realised she needed much more support than we had previously thought. This was a stark reality check and left us feeling angry and let down by her school.

Our elder daughter Connie found it impossible to tolerate any learning at home as, in her mind, home is home and school is school, and these have never been able to cross over. Her home was her sanctuary, not a place for demands or expectations. We had to adapt and find ways to keep her engaged and mentally stimulated without overwhelming her.

Ben was in his last year of school. He was due to sit his GCSEs and had been pushing back against any support or boundaries we put in place, and disengaged with this as a way to mask his lack of confidence in his ability. Football had been a huge part of his life, training three to four nights a week at weekends. And suddenly all that physical exercise and structure was wiped out overnight.

Our story of lockdown was like that of others in many ways, juggling home and the restrictions and anxiety of the pandemic. However, like many SEN families, we were doing it with fewer resources, more complexity, and rising fear. Food shopping turned into a nightmare when I couldn't get the specific foods our children relied on. I remember begging a supermarket worker to let me buy more baked beans (as this was the only brand our daughter would eat at the time), as foods become rationed for the world to ensure equity. They refused. So I queued again and again buying just enough to last the week, while balancing the risk of bringing home covid - and risking Chris as he was shielding.

Professionally, I was burning out. Emotionally I was on edge. I remember sitting on my bed during one NHS call about hospital capacity, hearing how patients would be prioritised by survival chance. I put the call on mute, rang my nan, and begged her not to answer the phone to anyone. I was terrified she'd be given a Do Not Attempt Cardiopulmonary Resuscitation (DNACPR) without understanding what it meant.

That was the turning point. I knew I couldn't keep going like this. And when my clinical supervisor suggested getting private sector experience if I wanted to move further up in leadership, I took the leap. I left the NHS.

The decision rocked me. The NHS had been my home, my identity. But values evolve. I still believe in equity and fairness – I always will – but I'd started to see how broken the system was. I started to develop a different perspective. Although the NHS is perceived to be free, it is simply paid for at source, out of the taxes we pay, but I couldn't invest in bits of healthcare that families like mine needed, and waiting lists were outrageous.

And I soon found out that working in the private sector showed me that with less red tape, more could be achieved. It changed how I thought about care, autonomy, and choice.

A Crash Course in Leadership

My new role as Head of Care in a retirement village was a crash course in leadership under pressure. We kept COVID at bay for a while, but within a few months, it had made its way in. One resident – living with dementia – tested positive, so we had to act. We created safe zones, kept people calm, and helped the team rally when it would've been easier to fall apart.

Then came vaccinations, which we had to roll out to residents and staff. I trained to deliver them myself, alongside the Village Manager and GP. People were understandably anxious and concerned about the impact that the vaccine might have. We started undertaking the mammoth task of vaccinating over 450 people. I had never felt more like a "proper nurse". It was terrifying and empowering. For all the doubts I had in my early career, here I was. Leading, supporting, showing up.

Nurse Kim

My dear colleague, who was the head of facilities, was by my side throughout this journey and provided me with moral support. I was so pleased to be able to offer her a role at Autism Oxford UK a year after I left the retirement village.

The CQC inspection came next, which was a challenging and rewarding experience. Something I learned during the NHS was that while you do absolutely need to know what you are doing, you also need to reach the right people and have the right rapport. When I was first in post, I had reached out to the CQC inspector for the area and introduced myself. I would email updates on what we were doing and innovative approaches we were implementing for those living with dementia.

So when the unannounced inspection happened my adrenaline kicked in. I thought we were doomed when the inspector stopped calling families halfway through their list. But no. They were just "fed up with hearing how good you are". We got a glowing review.

Residents and families were happier even despite the visiting restrictions the pandemic imposed. I had briefed my team and told them to do what they usually do and to highlight what great carers and nurses they are. I encouraged them to speak to the inspector and share ideas and constructive feedback. When we did the walk around the team looked confident and I was proud of every single one of them.

The inspector praised me for my leadership and for running a safe, caring and well-led service which had been responsive to residents and families in extremely difficult circumstances, and they provided us with an overall good rating. This was a significant accomplishment, given the circumstances. I cried in my car after work that day, out of pride and disbelief.

However, the ugly head of the private sector and finances rose in our weekly calls with the regional team. We were constantly pressured to fill beds even when it was not the right thing to do and make more money. Although we'd kept them at bay for a while, then came the instruction: raise all fees by 50 per cent.

I mean, 50 per cent! I listened to the justification and the impact on revenue that COVID-19 was having across all retirement villages, but why was it the residents' problem?

I couldn't do it. These were people's homes. They'd trusted us. And I wasn't going to be the one to break that. My integrity was too great, so I resigned. I handed in my resignation there and then, with no real thought as to how I was going to support my family or what Chris might say.

I had no plan. No job lined up. Just a deep belief that this wasn't right – and that something else would be.

When I got home and Chris asked me how my day had been, I casually dropped it into the conversation and walked off to get changed, hearing his gasp as I left the room. But I didn't flinch. Yes, it was a well-paid job. Yes, we relied on my income to cover the bills. But I knew we'd figure it out.

And we did. I reached out to old colleagues, picked up freelance work with an autism assessment provider, and slowly started rebuilding my specialist roots in autism and ADHD – while quietly laying the foundations for something of our own.

Because the truth is, not long before I walked away, I'd been given a strange and generous offer. And deep down, I already knew I was going to bet on myself. That made walking away easier. Not easy. But easier.

Finding Home in the Chaos

Not long before I handed in my notice, we had bought our first home. It was a dream come true, something we had never thought would be possible. We'd been in social housing for years, and the jump to a mortgage felt terrifying. The house was cheap, a bit broken, but big enough for our family of five – and more importantly, it could be adapted one day if Chris's health declined further.

It felt like a bold, grown-up decision. But it quickly became another weight I carried. Every room needed work. Money was tight. And despite our best intentions, the house is still not accessible for Chris when he's unwell. That guilt runs deep sometimes. But Chris always reminds me – this was *our* choice, *our* next chapter.

Despite the challenges, there were also moments of joy and pride. Each completed project brought a sense of achievement and progress. We celebrated the small victories, like finally having internal doors or finishing the children's bedrooms. These moments reminded us why we were doing this and kept us motivated to keep going.

We bought the house for security, but also for hope. And even on the hardest days, I try to remember: we're building something, slowly. Together.

Learning Point:

Your Values Are Your Anchor

The biggest storms aren't always external – sometimes they come from inside, when your identity shifts, your beliefs evolve, and your values are tested. The NHS shaped me. But it was stepping outside of it that showed me who I really was as a leader.

You don't have to follow the same path forever. You're allowed to change. And when the storm hits, your values will tell you what to do.

Chapter 9
Not Part of the Plan

"This was not the plan."

I've said those words more times than I can count. Usually to Chris, sitting in the kitchen feeling dazed after another long day, wondering how life turned out this way. But the truth is, I do know how it happened: I worked incredibly hard, I trusted my instincts, and I took brave, sometimes reckless, leaps – even when it felt like everything could fall apart.

AutismOxford
UK Limited

Autism Oxford UK was never part of the plan – but sometimes the most impactful ventures arise from the most unforeseen circumstances. And, if I'm honest, it's become one of the best decisions of my life, even if it didn't always feel like it at the time.

The Call That Changed Everything

It started with a phone call. The previous owner of Autism Oxford UK was preparing to wind the organisation down. She'd been in discussions with the National Autistic Society – who, at the time, were an autistic-led training provider – to see if they'd take it on. But she was worried the heart of the organisation would be lost. That it would disappear inside a much larger system and lose the identity it had been built on.

But her call wasn't just to tell me that. She had something else in mind. She'd got wind that I had recently left the NHS and reached out to ask if I might be interested in buying the organisation. I was gobsmacked. "Why me?" I asked. I was dumbfounded that someone would think I was capable of running a business. But she reassured me that she felt I was the right person.

She remembered my work from the NHS – my advocacy and my fierce belief in doing things differently. She also knew I had two autistic children. To her, that blend of lived and professional experience made me the ideal person to take it forward.

But I had to be brutally honest with her. There had been too many other things going on. We'd just bought our first house, Chris had recently medically retired, and – at the time of the offer – I was only a few months into a new job. There was no way I could afford something like this. I thanked her, and we left it there.

Our first house

Making the Impossible Decision

We parted ways, but a week later, she called again. This time she opened with, "I've been thinking. Getting Autism Oxford UK into the right hands is more important than money." And then she offered to gift me the business.

I was sitting in a car park at work when the call came through, trying to keep the signal while my heart did somersaults and my brain spiralled through all the what-ifs. I rang Chris, my stepmum, my dad, and my former boss. The responses were mixed – some people were excited, others thought I was mad. My former boss said she'd support me through the early stages if I went ahead.

So I stopped thinking and went with my gut. And I picked up the phone and said yes, accepting the opportunity.

My uncle, who owned a successful trade business, came to visit soon after. We sat together over a cup of tea while he reassured me about the journey I was about to take – but he also prepared me for failure. He shared a stark truth: 70 per cent of startups fail within the first five years, often due to cash flow issues. That message stayed with me. Despite the warnings being loud and clear – and me being clueless – we started to try and work it out.

Thrown In the Deep End

It wasn't long before the panic set in. I had no idea what I was doing. I actually had to Google "due diligence" because I didn't have a clue what it meant. Looking back, I cringe when I realised how much I didn't know. I muddled my way through past business accounts. I asked about work in the pipeline (although I didn't call it that back then). Luckily, my dad's accountant stepped in and supported us through the process, and we worked towards a handover date of 1 December 2020. Everything seemed in order.

Then, on the day of handover, the previous owner emptied the business account – a final payment she felt she was owed. Legally, she could do it, but we hadn't expected it. There were bills to pay, and we were left with nothing in the account. It was terrifying. We had no money, no backup, and no time to dwell. We just had to get on with it.

After the handover, we had to figure out how to run a business, both of us novices and green, not really having a clue where to even start. We thanked the invention of the internet, which in that moment became our best friend, providing us with help in the form of the "dummies, guide to running a business".

We had to start from scratch. Despite the warnings being loud and clear – and being clueless – Chris took the lead in researching accounting systems, websites, and everything in between.

I'd committed to running the organisation and, despite the shaky start, I wasn't going to back down, and the idea of Autism Oxford UK began to take shape.

Finding a Mentor and Saying Yes Again

Starting a business was a daunting task, especially one that required such an elevated level of expertise and sensitivity. I didn't have any formal business training. I didn't know what I didn't know. I just knew I couldn't mess this up. I needed help.

I started reaching out to business mentors, hoping to find someone who could help me work out how to actually structure this thing and create something sustainable. But no one really clicked initially. Until I met James Martin. He was a little corporate for my liking, a bit too blunt – but he *got it*. He understood my vision. He listened to me and pitched me his growth plan. He said, "You could do this on your own, but you'll do it faster with me." I like fast!

Chris was nervous and worried about whether we could afford the fees. Understandably so. We had barely enough money as it was, and now I wanted to spend more on a business mentor?

I love how he continues to question every crazy idea I produce, but I knew deep down this was something I had to try. So I said yes again. And that yes, like the first one, changed everything.

Investing in mentorship at all stages of my journey has been transformative, and James became a guiding force, helping me to understand how to run a business, and take off my "NHS hat", and he provided unwavering support through the challenges I have faced. He taught me about financial management, marketing and how to sell yourself (a completely new concept to me!), strategic planning, and the importance of building a strong team. His guidance helped me navigate the complexities of the business world and provided me with the tools, confidence and resilience I needed to succeed.

Learning Point:
Say Yes Before You're Ready

Some of the best journeys begin with fear, followed by a hesitant yes. You don't need a perfect plan – just the courage to start, the humility to learn, and the resilience to keep going.

If you are running a business, it will be challenging at times and there will be times when you feel overwhelmed. If you feel this way, stay focused on your mission and remember why you started. Resilience and perseverance are key to overcoming adversity.

Also, building a business is not a solo endeavour. Reach out to your network, seek advice from mentors, and do not be afraid to ask for help. Collaboration and support are crucial to success and they will help you to navigate the complexities of doing something new.

Chapter 10
Growing Autism Oxford UK

"Don't do it," people told me constantly. "It'll burn you out." But I did it anyway.

When we started Autism Oxford UK in December 2020, we were literally sitting at our kitchen table with one laptop, wondering where to even begin. In the early days, I was also working two other jobs so we could keep our heads above water.

Before I took it on, the organisation had been activist-led and run entirely by volunteers. I respected the work that had been done before me, but I've always believed that people should be paid for their time

CEO 'Kimberley'

and expertise. That was a value I couldn't let go of. But there was no money, we were still mid-pandemic, and we had nothing to fall back on.

In a strange way, the timing helped. Being new to business, we did not have the financial means to afford a physical premises, and the shift to online services meant we could operate without the overhead costs of a physical location, and no one was expecting in-person events or office space, which was a significant relief to get us going.

We built our services online from day one, which – alongside the lower overheads – gave us broader reach. This allowed us to focus our resources on building our team and reaching more families. Now, as we have grown, we have needed premises, but at the start, this was a blessing in disguise.

Losing Credibility – And Finding It Again

I began by setting the vision and what we were going to do – what we were going to offer. I knew the gaps in services for autistic adults. I had spent three years in my past NHS role fighting and campaigning for services for these individuals. The challenge, though, was that we were not commissioned to provide services, and there was no money in the system.

The other challenge I hadn't realised I'd face was the change in attitude and people's views of me, simply because I did not work in the NHS anymore. Only my lanyard had changed but it felt so much more than that.

Suddenly, people I had worked hard to build relationships with treated me differently. That was a shock. I hadn't realised how much credibility came from the institution I worked for, and the moment that badge was gone, so was their trust. It hurt. When I was in the NHS, I hadn't realised how institutionalised it was or how damaging that actually is.

Nevertheless, I connected with the few who had not shut me out – people who had also left the system. I pulled on all the people and knowledge I had and started to piece an offering together.

I wanted to ensure we broke down as many barriers as possible. Age and neurodivergence were the big ones. After all, people don't grow out of being autistic or having ADHD – so why do we have an age separation in services for these communities?

I searched through my predecessor's mailbox and reached out to others who had connected with her. One of those contacts paid off, and they became a dear colleague and someone who helped trailblaze the start of Autism Oxford UK with me, alongside two ex-colleagues.

It wasn't a grand vision at first as we were all working other jobs but we had a shared dream and we built Autism Oxford UK bit by bit. We started small. Initially, it was just consultations and a couple of small workshops. But as soon as we added assessments, the demand exploded. We didn't realise how quickly things would grow. Word spread far quicker than I'd imagined, and I started receiving enquiries from all over the country. I felt like I was spinning so many plates, and any moment, one might fall and smash everything to pieces.

Chris kept me grounded, but I knew we had to take risks. Playing it safe wasn't going to build what I knew this organisation could be. Every decision we made stirred up my deepest

childhood fears – fear of losing everything, of dragging my family into poverty, of failing. But instead of paralysing me, those fears became my fuel.

Chris and Kim

Team Growth

Once Chris and I had moved on from our shared laptop, we became a team of four, working evenings and weekends. This soon became a team of ten, then twelve. Up until then we'd all been self-employed, just making it work. But it wasn't sustainable. Eventually, I made the call to put people on payroll.

Chris was anxious. Of course he was. These were people who had walked away from job security to follow a vision – my vision. And suddenly, we were responsible for their rent and their mortgages. That responsibility hit me like a ton of bricks. I'm sure they believed in us more than we believed in ourselves at this point!

We brought new team members on board, one by one, as the vision grew and the work demanded more hands. The financial growth matched the workforce growth, and the need for space grew alongside it. We are still growing – and growing at pace.

When we hit 50 team members, the reality of what we were building truly hit me. That was 50 lives we were responsible for, 50 people depending on the decisions we made. It was exciting – but terrifying. I finally understood Chris's early anxiety. We were no longer playing at this. This was people's livelihoods. And that pressure has always stayed with me. The sleepless nights, the shift from "we're just trying this out" to "this is real – this is people's lives" hit like a tidal wave.

It has made me work harder, think deeper, and never take any of it for granted. I now use that weight to drive me, just as I did with the anxiety around failing and thrusting my family into poverty. Failure was never an option. The question is never "Will this work?" but always "How will we get this to work?"

There have been many times on my journey when I have wondered why on earth people should follow me. I guess it's my imposter narrative, but I am passionate and a good nurse too. You'd have imagined that, given my background, the growth and leadership challenges would have been more complex to me, but I have always been pro leadership over management. I believe when you lead you get so much more out of people over managing them – after all, I work with fully grown adults who are autonomous in their lives, why on earth would I want to try and manage that? I wanted to create something different.

Creating a New Kind of Organisation

In just four years, Autism Oxford UK had transformed from me and Chris in our kitchen into a thriving organisation with a team of 50 dedicated professionals. Our revenue had skyrocketed from a modest £10,000 to an impressive £1.2 million, then £2 million in 2025. This rapid growth is a testament to our success and the increasing demand for our services. However, such swift expansion has also presented significant challenges that require careful management and strategic planning.

Rapid growth, while exciting, can be a double-edged sword. It brings opportunities for increased revenue, market share, and influence, but it also comes with its own set of challenges. These challenges can be broadly categorised into several key areas: scaling operations, talent acquisition and retention, maintaining company culture, internal controls and operational structures, and clear communication and strategic planning.

To illustrate these points, let us delve into Autism Oxford UK's growth journey. As I have already mentioned, when we started, we were a small operation with a big vision. Our mission was to provide high-quality support and services to individuals with autism and their families. As demand for our services grew, we faced the challenge of scaling our operations while maintaining our commitment to excellence. We invested in technology to streamline our processes and improve efficiency. One such example was how we leveraged technology to enhance accessibility. Our online assessments and telehealth consultations allowed us to reach families across the UK, breaking down geographical barriers. Virtual workshops and support groups provided a sense of community and connection, even during the isolation of the pandemic.

Steve Jobs, co-founder of Apple, emphasised the importance of teamwork in a strong culture and said, *"Great things in business are never done by one person. They're done by a team of people."*[4] This highlights how a collaborative environment can drive innovation and success.

I knew that organisational culture is a critical component of any successful business. It defines your company's internal and external identity, guiding employees in their daily interactions and decision-making processes. A strong organisational culture promotes a positive, structured work environment that helps companies succeed. It increases employee engagement, decreases turnover, elevates productivity, and strengthens brand identity.

To recruit and retain the right people, building a strong employer brand was a priority. We highlighted our mission and values in our recruitment efforts, attracting individuals who were passionate about making a difference. Competitive compensation packages and opportunities for professional development helped us retain top talent.

As our team grew, we made a conscious effort to maintain our company culture. Regular team meetings, open communication, and celebrating successes were key to fostering a positive and

---

4 Source: https://www.brainyquote.com/quotes/steve_jobs_737723.

inclusive environment. We established robust financial controls and developed Standard Operating Procedures (SOPs) for key processes. Monitoring Key Performance Indicators (KPIs) allowed us to track performance and make informed decisions. Developing a strategic plan was crucial. We communicated our vision and goals to all employees, ensuring alignment and fostering a collaborative environment.

I knew that organisations with a strong work culture are appealing for job candidates looking for a permanent position and the opportunity for growth. It motivates everyone to do their best work, creating an atmosphere of positivity that is hard to ignore. It also helps retain top talent, as people who feel valued and respected at a company are more likely to stay. A well-functioning culture assists with onboarding, transforming employees into advocates for the company. It fosters a sense of belonging and purpose, driving productivity and performance levels overall.

Managing rapid growth is a complex and challenging endeavour, but with careful planning and strategic execution, it is possible to navigate these challenges successfully.

By focusing on these areas, Autism Oxford UK has been able to sustain its growth and continue making a positive impact. For other entrepreneurs facing similar challenges, remember that growth is a journey. Stay true to your mission, invest in your people, and continuously seek opportunities for improvement. With the right strategies and mindset, you can turn the challenges of rapid growth into opportunities for long-term success.

The impact of these innovations was profound. Families reported feeling more supported and understood, and our client satisfaction rates soared. We received countless messages of gratitude from parents who had finally found the help they needed after years of struggling within the system.

Go Big or Go Home

Autism Oxford UK's impact has been immense. The overwhelming demand for autism and ADHD services in the UK was both a challenge and a call to action. Waiting lists were – and continue to be – one of the most significant barriers for families seeking support. We have worked tirelessly to reduce waiting times and provide post-diagnostic support, filling a critical gap in the system.

Here's just one statistic I read: "*Since 2019, there has been a five-fold rise in people waiting to see an autism specialist and a 51% increase in prescriptions for ADHD medication, according to the Nuffield Trust. Growing backlogs and longer waiting times are negatively impacting people's daily lives."[5]*

One of the initiatives I am most proud of is our emphasis on family-centred care. We recognised that supporting neurodivergent individuals requires a holistic approach that includes their families. By offering peer support, training, workshops, and resources for parents and caregivers, we aimed to empower families to navigate their journeys with confidence.

And now we have moved from just supporting autistic adults, to supporting all ages and all neurodivergence across assessments, therapies, peer support, consultancy, and training. Most organisations would focus on one of these areas and they are all viable business ventures in their own right – but in true Kim fashion of "go big or go home", the ambition is to provide everything a neurodivergent individual needs in one place.

We have successfully launched the Ashwin–Baker[6] model – blending lived experience and clinical expertise. It brings together two worlds

---

5 Jessica Morris, *The Rapidly Growing Waiting Lists for Autism and ADHD Assessments*, Nuffield Trust, 4 April 2024.

6 Chloe Baker is a Speech and Language Therapist who developed this.

that are often at conflict with one another due to the perceived hierarchy on each side. We've worked hard to neutralise that and remove hierarchy from care models entirely. This has helped us build back our credibility within the institutionalised NHS and show that there is a better way – one that genuinely benefits our neurodivergent community: my family.

It has also enabled us to offer meaningful employment to neurodivergent individuals, in a workplace where I hope they can be their authentic selves. But for me, this still doesn't feel like enough. My next campaign is to work out how we remove the financial barriers for individuals needing our services – people like my family – while still ensuring we are commercially successful. I know those two things often conflict, but I'll keep pushing to find a way. Because it's the right thing to do.

During this period, I started devouring business books – Sara Davies and Steven Bartlett were hugely influential for me. Steven Bartlett's *Happy Sexy Millionaire* gave me the idea for a bold PR move, which is another example of go big or go home. Steven installed a blue slide in his office. I went one better: I bought a bus. A big one. With a slide (thank you Steven).

At first, people thought I'd lost the plot and wondered what on earth I was doing. But then I explained it. I had a vision: to create a sensory-

Autism Oxford bus

friendly mobile space for the team and a safe play space for young children with SEN. It was also a great PR and marketing tool, and a conversation starter. It was bold. It was different. And it worked. Our first TikTok got over 50,000 views. The bus became a brand symbol, and it did exactly what I needed it to do.

The Reality Behind the Growth

I spent the first four years of Autism Oxford UK conflicted in where I spent my time. Asking myself questions like "Where can I have the biggest impact for our community?" I have still not managed to reach this conclusion and continue to blend "Nurse Kim" with "CEO Mum", with "Little Kim" in the background looking over these two, trying to ensure we do not become another failed business statistic.

"Little Kim"

Our growth, despite my being dyslexic and not really having an understanding of business, has excited me – and it's good to have strategies and systems in place to support it, alongside my acquired business knowledge and a trusted business mentor. But becoming the CEO of a fast-growing organisation required more than operational learning. It demanded that I grow into a different version of myself – and that part wasn't so easy.

I hadn't expected that being a woman would shape my leadership experience so profoundly.

When I worked in the NHS, I never felt my gender was a barrier. I assumed that in today's world, hard work and passion would speak for themselves. But outside the system, I was forced to reckon with how deeply credibility is tied to appearances, tone, and outdated expectations.

At times, I felt invisible. I found myself being talked over, underestimated, or simply not taken seriously – subtle things that added up. People assumed Chris was in charge. I was asked if there was someone "more senior" they could speak to. I questioned whether I needed to change how I dressed or presented myself – just to be heard.

I tried for a while. I experimented with corporate polish. But it felt wrong. Over time, I realised I didn't need to lead like anyone else. I needed to lead like me. I started to own my voice, not soften it. I embraced the fact that I bring empathy, instinct, and heart to the table – and that those things are not weaknesses. They are my edge. I built a culture where others didn't have to code-switch or perform professionalism to belong. And that meant starting with myself.

That was the real growth. Not just operational or strategic, but personal. Deep. Uncomfortable. Transformational.

But that growth came with a cost. And the toll of carrying it would show itself very soon.

Learning Point:

Growth Is Heavy, But Worth It

The biggest growth wasn't financial. It was personal. I had to grow into the leader this organisation needed – someone who could hold the vision, take the risks, and carry the weight of other people's livelihoods. That transformation didn't come overnight, and it didn't come without cost.

There were days I doubted everything – my decisions, my abilities, even my right to lead. I've cried in the car, panicked about payroll, and wondered how I was going to keep all the plates spinning. But I've also felt the pride of watching my team flourish, of seeing the lives we've impacted, and of building something that matters. That's what keeps me going. That's why it's worth it.

Chapter 11
Descending Into Darkness

Note that this is an intense chapter. Please refer to the Trigger Warning at the beginning of this book. Take care while reading. It's OK to pause, skip, or reach out for help if you need it.

"*E*veryone is better off without me. I am just hurting everyone."

This thought would get bigger and bigger until it overtook all my thoughts, and I made the decision to try and act on this thought. And I almost ended my own life.

I was used to facing challenges, but there was a period in my life when the weight of it all became too much to bear, and the chronic state of the year weighed too heavily, which led into a descent into darkness and massively impacted my mental wellbeing.

Running Autism Oxford UK was a dream that I did not even realise I had – something that doesn't happen to people like me. But with dreams, there is a reality of immense hardship and sacrifices that are needed, along with incredible pressure.

Kim

My life has always been demanding due to the nature of the multiple hats I wear: mum, SEN mum, wife, daughter, sister, CEO, nurse, but these hats suddenly felt so heavy, and were too much to wear with the added turmoil of the year that unfolded and the challenge to my character – to my identity. I felt a constant need to prove myself, to be strong for my team and my family, leaving little room for vulnerability. I felt like I was walking a tightrope, and any misstep could lead to disaster.

The Breaking Point

The breaking point came three years into running the organisation. I faced my first litigation claim, was accused of harassment, stalking, and discrimination against the very community I had dedicated my career to supporting, all in the space of three months. This left no time to come up for air and bounce back from each battering.

What felt like a personal attack began with a police complaint, followed by a complaint within Autism Oxford UK about my conduct, and a Subject Access Request (SAR) demanding data from over 50,000 emails and several WhatsApp exchanges. This unreasonable and malicious request crippled our small organisation, both in terms of time and financial resources and there was nothing I could do. I felt so helpless.

The situation escalated with an anonymous complaint to the Care Quality Commission (CQC) for allegedly completing regulated activities while unregulated alongside a Nursing and Midwifery Council (NMC) investigation for fitness to practise, both of which were later found to be unfounded.

This was followed by an employment tribunal application accusing me of being a danger to disabled people.

The CQC Investigation

The investigation brought our successful growth to a screeching halt, forcing us to pause services, make redundancies, and shift our focus from growth to mere survival. I felt personally responsible for people losing their jobs. It did not matter what people were saying around me – telling me it was not my fault, that I had not done anything wrong. While the facts indicated this was true in some part, the other part was that this would not have happened if it wasn't me in the position of CEO, and it felt like this was part of a wider attack on me.

The CQC, as the independent regulator of health and social care services in England, is responsible for ensuring that care providers meet essential standards of quality and safety. Their role includes monitoring, inspecting, and regulating services to ensure they meet these fundamental standards. Despite several reassurances from the CQC that we did not need to be regulated, an investigator insisted otherwise. This discrepancy created significant confusion and uncertainty within our organisation.

The investigation process was exhaustive. It involved multiple conversations with solicitors, the investigator, extensive documentation, and numerous meetings with my team to try and stabilise and reassure them, during a time when I was not feeling assured myself. The stress and anxiety caused by the investigation were immense, affecting not only me but also my entire team.

Financially, the costs associated with legal fees, compliance measures, and potential fines were substantial. We had to allocate significant resources to address the investigation, diverting funds from other critical areas of the business. This financial strain forced us to make tough decisions, including pausing services and making redundancies. The uncertainty surrounding the investigation also affected our ability to secure new contracts and partnerships, further exacerbating our financial challenges.

Operationally, the investigation disrupted our daily activities and hindered our ability to focus on growth and innovation. We had to dedicate considerable time and effort to comply with the CQC's demands, which took a toll on our productivity and efficiency. The constant scrutiny and pressure from the investigation created a tense and stressful work environment, impacting team morale and cohesion. The uncertainty about our future created a pervasive sense of anxiety and stress. The investigation also triggered feelings of self-doubt and imposter syndrome, as I questioned my ability to lead the organisation through such a challenging period.

These experiences will stay with me for the rest of my life – in the words from the film *Inside Out*, they have become "core memories". I vividly remember the feeling of hopelessness, paired with sheer panic, while battling the sleepless nights, the endless meetings, amplified with the overwhelming sense of dread that accompanied each new development in the investigation.

There were moments when I felt utterly defeated, questioning whether I had made the right decision in taking on Autism Oxford UK, and my inner critic turned into my inner attacker, mocking me for thinking I could do this – that I could run a business and help people. The weight of responsibility felt crushing, and the fear of letting down my team and the families we serve was ever-present.

Red Flags

It was 3am in the morning and two colleagues and I were on a Teams call pulling all the documents together for the CQC. Chris was at home with our children, but also working well into the night trawling through thousands of emails for the SARS request. I got in my car to head home and just broke down. Emotions of guilt, shame, panic, and overwhelm all in one big ball.

I also was puzzled as to why people were helping. Why did people think I was worthy of the help? I have always strived for independence and people in my experience have never been consistent or reliable, so this felt like an alien experience. Not only did two colleagues sit with me at 3am in the morning (not being paid, I will add), but also team members rallied round and went above and beyond. Colleagues and system partners all pulled together and offered their support through endorsements for the NMC and CQC, giving us time and space to talk safely. And even those who did not know what to do, would simply bring me a cup of tea.

I am still to this day in awe and puzzled at how and why people gave me so much. When I say to them that I am indebted to them, they simply reply, "Maybe we are repaying our debt to you?"

Now I look back and think what an amazing thing to say and do. But at the time, this just made me feel more worthless and my inner attacker twisted these words, tainting them to shame me: "Ah, see, you owe them now – you made them feel that they had to pay you back." The mind is very clever and can be your best friend or your worst enemy.

The darkness continued to creep in, and the enemy in my mind was winning, turning passing comments from others into facts and negative evidence to back up its narrative that everyone would be better off without me. It was feeding itself, and became bigger and bigger. It provided a layer of shame, preventing me from speaking out and sharing these thoughts with others – spinning the narrative that people will think I am weak, or that they will affirm the inner attacker's words.

As a nurse, I should have noticed the red flags but I didn't. I faced a drop in mood and sense of hopelessness. I would tell myself I was worthless and felt like I was a risk to others. I couldn't make even the simplest of decisions.

Alongside this, I organised my affairs, put life assurance in place, sorted my will and had started handing over the children's SEN coordination work and medical appointments. To the outside, my mood appeared to improve when we went on holiday, but this simply affirmed that my family and team would be fine and could manage without me.

I started to cut off friends and family that meant the world to me – ignoring phone calls and cancelling plans. I was ashamed of myself, but I was running on empty and just trying to survive. I had nothing left to give.

I was so poorly, but I didn't realise it. I had started to make unconscious plans to end my own life. I held on until one day I received an email from the NMC saying the complainant had asked for a second review. So they were reopening the fitness to practise investigation.

I simply got up, took the dog, and went to end my own life.

I turned my phone tracker off, and Chris called the police. He was concerned, especially knowing I'd received that email. He had an inkling that I wasn't right and was worried about my mental health. Luckily the police took it seriously, found me and brought me home. They had a photo and came across me walking down the road. A very gentle female officer walked me home because I refused to get in the police car.

Chris told the kids he had lost me and that was why the police were there, which helped them, and they were none the wiser. Looking back now, the thought of causing harm to my children, of them experiencing anything like what I had endured in my childhood, was unbearable. But I was broken. I felt like a failure, and the weight of that belief was suffocating.

My Safety Plan

In the midst of this darkness, Chris became my safety plan. He thought for me, made decisions over basic life choices, and provided the structure I desperately needed. I could not trust myself or my inner thoughts, but I could trust him. He was my protector and decision-maker. He saved my life, alongside my clinical psychologist who I had started seeing to try and make all this go away.

Chris made specific decisions for me, such as:

- Ensuring I ate regularly: Chris would prepare meals and remind me to eat, knowing that I often neglected my nutrition when overwhelmed by stress.

- Managing my sleep schedule: He made space along with colleagues in my diary for me to sleep. I have never slept so much in my life – this was a safe space for me, my mind would switch off, and I could feel like I could breathe.

- Attending therapy sessions: Chris ensured my laptop was ready and I had a private space for my therapy sessions. He would not pry afterwards, but would greet me with a small smile and a cup of tea.

- Making daily life choices: From deciding what I should wear to managing household tasks, Chris took over these decisions to reduce my mental load and reassuring me, it's OK, that I'm OK.

- Providing emotional support: He was always there to listen, offer comfort, and reassure me during moments of self-doubt and despair. His presence provided a sense of stability and safety that I could not find within myself.

Safety planning is a crucial strategy for individuals experiencing severe emotional distress and while I was breathing I was not living. It involves creating a structured plan to ensure safety and wellbeing during times of crisis. For me, Chris was the cornerstone of this plan. He monitored my mental state, intervened when necessary, and provided the emotional support I needed to navigate this challenging period.

With Chris's support and the help of my clinical psychologist, I slowly began to rebuild myself. It was a long and painful process, but it was also a journey of rediscovery and resilience. Chris's unwavering belief in me gave me the strength to keep going, even when I felt like giving up.

Kim

Alongside this, I put other grounding techniques in place. I had a jar of pennies that my brother had put his body spray in; this was something he had had growing up, which I got off him as payment for going to the shop with him. He also put together a photo slideshow for my desk at work.

My work colleagues covered my diary and pulled my revalidation file for nursing which had in it all the compliments and feedback and thank-you cards from my career. Piece by piece people rebuilt me.

Not long after this, I had to get through the CQC interview, which was so physically hard, but we passed with flying colours. We achieved CQC registration, only to be told that we did not need it for our current offerings. While the charges were dropped, the lasting impact on myself and the team was significant. But it helped me to rebuild. It reaffirmed that I was not a bad person.

Bit by bit, things changed. And the NMC closed the fitness to practise claim again.

Emerging Stronger

While all of this was happening, the employment tribunal was going on. A year later, the tribunal judge dismissed the claim, but the financial impact and emotional turmoil were significant, and the scars still remain. This experience underscored the importance of having a strong support system and seeking professional help when needed. The litigation not only drained our financial resources but also affected our ability to focus on growth and innovation. It was a stark reminder of the potential risks and challenges that come with running a business.

In retrospect, the CQC investigation was a challenging and painful experience, but it also provided valuable lessons. It reinforced the importance of compliance protocols to ensure we meet all regulatory requirements and avoid similar issues in the future. This includes regular audits, staff training, and ongoing communication with regulatory bodies to stay informed about any changes in regulations.

It also highlighted the need for resilience and adaptability in the face of adversity. Despite the difficulties, we emerged stronger and more prepared to navigate the complexities of the healthcare sector.

Descending into the darkness was one of the most harrowing experiences of my life. It tested my resilience, my strength, and my will to continue. But it also taught me the importance of vulnerability, of asking for help, and of leaning on those who care about you. It reminded me that even in the darkest moments, there is hope and a way forward.

Chris's role as my safety plan was a lifeline that saved my life. His unwavering support, decision-making, and emotional presence provided the stability I needed to navigate the darkest period of my life.

As for the team, it actually brought us together closer. The support, solidarity, and determination displayed by everyone at Autism Oxford UK were truly inspiring. Our open communication kept everyone informed, addressed concerns, and maintained trust. Together, we navigated the storm and emerged stronger, more resilient, and more united than ever before.

Learning Point:

However Deep the Darkness, There Is Always a Path to the Light

This chapter is a testament to the power of support, resilience, and the human spirit. It is a reminder that no matter how deep the darkness, there is always a path to the light. And it is a call to anyone who is struggling to reach out, to seek help, and to believe that they are not alone.

While this has been a harrowing part of my life, this is where my biggest growth has happened. Those around me as I descended into darkness told me it would all be OK and I would come out stronger. While at the time I did not hear this, I do now see this.

If you are in the darkness please seek support, please remember you are not alone, and there is always more than one solution.

Chapter 12
Striving for Independence

"*I* am not interested in money, I want independence."

The final tribunal date in January 2025 marked the end of a brutal chapter. I remember sitting staring at the virtual meeting room screen as I said this to myself. It felt like groundhog day. My day of reckoning.

I had met with my barrister and solicitor ahead of time, who reassured me that I am a nice human, but my palms were still sweating as I waited for the decision. It wasn't just a legal process, it was a reckoning. When the verdict came, I didn't feel relief. I felt hollow. The battle was over, but the war inside me had already blown me apart and now I had a long journey ahead of me – piecing myself back together.

My journey had never been about the money or a "get rich quick" crusade – it's about reaching independence, going back to 16-year-old Kim, who knew she needed to make things happen for herself – that's all I wanted to do, and all this had brought this into question. Had I had taken the right path or not? After such a traumatic year it really did place things into perspective and ironically, while I have strived for independence, these circumstances led to me more dependent than I have ever been.

The Road to Recovery

Although I was emerging stronger, there were times when recovery felt like a never-ending battle. The emotional and psychological toll was insurmountable, but it also forced me to confront my deepest fears and insecurities. I had to learn to trust myself, to believe that I was capable of leading and making a difference.

There were days when getting out of bed seemed impossible. The weight of imposter syndrome was heavy, constantly whispering that I wasn't good enough, that I didn't belong. "Little Kim" in my mind was having a nervous breakdown, as all the strategies she'd developed to keep me safe in childhood – which had served me well in adulthood until now – no longer worked.

But I've learned that recovery isn't a linear process. It's messy, it's painful, and it's filled with setbacks. But it's also filled with moments of growth and self-discovery. They've challenged me to reflect deeply on who I am, what I stand for, and how I show up in the world – not just as a CEO or a nurse, but as Kimberley.

Independence versus Financial Stability

Reflecting on the journey that has brought me to this point, I'm reminded of the countless challenges and triumphs that have shaped my path from a teen mum to the CEO of Autism Oxford UK. Each chapter of my life has been a testament to resilience, determination, and the unwavering pursuit of independence – not just for myself, but for my family and the community I serve.

This also means striving for financial stability, as I can't have independence without the financial stability, and I'm learning this isn't a dirty ambition to have, nor does it resemble greed. The learning continues and I long for the day where I'm truly independent and no longer rely on others but can be the one relied on. I've always wanted to create a life where I can make decisions that align with my values and aspirations, and no one can let me down. It's about providing a secure and nurturing environment for my family and empowering others to achieve their potential. I'm filled with a profound sense of gratitude and determination.

Independence means having the freedom to pursue my passions and make a positive impact on the world. It means building a sustainable organisation that can continue to support families and individuals for years to come. It means breaking free from the constraints of self-doubt and societal expectations and forging a path that is uniquely my own.

As Karren Brady once said, "The one thing I wanted was independence. And I realised to have that independence, you needed financial independence."[7] That quote resonates deeply with my journey.

I've never been financially or materially driven. I've just been driven by an assurance that my family's basic needs – food, shelter, living without

---

[7]   Karren Brady, *Strong Woman: The Truth About Getting to the Top* (HarperCollins, 2012).

fear of harm – can be met. These are simple but often taken for granted. If you can create these, you also create independence and security. Running your own business gives you space to achieve this. You are the one in charge of the success – or not. You make decisions about the team around you, the culture and the drive for growth. You set the pace and tone. While I've talked about these being an overwhelming burden, they also represent independence and autonomy.

This is an independence I had never experienced before. When you work for someone else, you always have to report in. Even if they allow you autonomy, it will be clipped to fit their vision and wants.

Within independence, there is a need for confidence – something I haven't always had internally but often portray externally. You need to be confident in your decision-making and confident in leading a workforce. You also need confidence that some of your decisions won't be popular and you will lose people on your journey. I've been pretty comfortable with the first two, but the latter is one that has taken some time, and can still be a hurdle for me.

While I wouldn't describe myself as a people pleaser, I do gain great personal reward from helping others. My childhood adversity taps into "Little Kim", the hypervigilant little girl in me trying to keep me safe and foresee any dangers. This strategy helped me survive when I was younger. It's led to me adapting to people or situations around me to avoid confrontation or conflict. At times, that's been helpful – but it's not so effective in adulthood when striving for true independence.

It would be easy to rush in and try to work on my confidence, thinking that's the issue. But that would be superficial. The real need is to work through the trauma and process my childhood experiences to build that confidence. I need to support "Little Kim", to build her confidence that we're OK – in fact, more than OK – and that we don't need to deploy those old, reliable strategies anymore. There is another way...

I've started compassion-focused therapy to support this. When I tell people, they look puzzled, as I'm often seen as a compassionate person – and indeed, as a nurse, I should be. And I am – to others. But not always to myself. This has been an enlightening experience. I'm building resilience in accepting compliments rather than diminishing them with a humorous comment or throwing a compliment right back. This is building my confidence in being who I am and want to be, and edging me closer to that golden independence.

Learning Point:

The Road to Independence Is Paved With Self-Compassion

I want to leave you with a message of hope and encouragement. No matter where you are in your journey, know that you have the strength and resilience to overcome any obstacle. Embrace the unexpected opportunities, celebrate your firsts, and turn self-doubt into a driving force for growth. Surround yourself with a strong support system and never be afraid to ask for help.

Striving for independence is a lifelong journey, but it is one filled with immense rewards. Believe in yourself, stay true to your values, and keep pushing forward. You have the power to create a life of purpose, fulfilment, and independence.

Chapter 13
Personal Growth

"People like me don't write books."

I said this to James, my business mentor, when he suggested I write this one.

I am dyslexic, and dyslexic people don't write books. That was the sort of message that was reinforced throughout my childhood, especially through the words my mum used to my brother: "You're stupid, you're thick." He was severely dyslexic, and I absorbed those words too. My own dyslexia wasn't even identified until university.

I can read (albeit slowly) and I can kind of spell (the team will often comment that you'll find "Kim-isms" throughout my work). But it's hard.

I have no phonological knowledge whatsoever.[8] In childhood, I learned to adapt and camouflaged to survive.

Imposter Syndrome

Imposter syndrome has followed me like a quiet shadow throughout much of this journey and it's a term that resonates with many high-achieving individuals. Despite my accomplishments and the positive impact I have had on countless lives, there are moments when I feel like a fraud, waiting for someone to call me out.

I used to think imposter syndrome was something I had to get over. But I've come to realise it's just a signpost. A sign that I care deeply about the work I do.

Sara Davies, in her *6 Minute Entrepreneur* podcast, offers an insightful take on managing imposter syndrome. She reminds herself that others have made the decision for her to be in the position she's in – like being a Dragon on *Dragons'*

---

8 Research shows that dyslexia is strongly linked to deficits in phonological awareness – the ability to recognise and manipulate the sound structures of language. This phonological need affects the development of reading skills across languages.

Den. That really resonated with me. It shifts the focus from self-doubt to recognising the confidence others have in you. And that can be incredibly grounding.

What has shifted is how I respond to it. Instead of listening to that inner critic, I remind myself of everything I've survived, everything I've built, and everyone who believes in me – even when I've struggled to believe in myself. I still have wobbles, but I don't let them stop me. That's the difference.

For me, imposter syndrome has pushed me to step out of my comfort zone and embrace opportunities that I might have otherwise shied away from. I am stretching myself. I am not playing small.

Why Did I Write a Book?

Now, you might be wondering – given my dyslexia and the doubt that has lingered throughout my life – why would I decide to write a book?

Well, here's the thing. Throughout this journey, I've learned that people write books because they have something meaningful to say. It's about sharing something that might help or inspire others. It's about truth and helping others feel seen. It's *not* about being able to spell every word. That shift in perspective changed everything. Reframing it turned something I'd never dreamed of doing into something achievable.

Sure, the process of drafting this book was challenging. There were times when I doubted myself and felt overwhelmed by the task. However, I was determined to push through and to share my story. I sought out support from mentors and colleagues, who provided guidance and encouragement. I also took the time to reflect on my journey, to understand my strengths and weaknesses.

Writing this book has been cathartic and a healing process, a bold step, and an act of hope. It has stretched me more than I ever imagined. But it's also helped me reflect on my journey and shown me just how far I've come. And, if you've made it this far, thank you.

I didn't write it because I had all the answers. I wrote it because I believe stories can open doors. If even one part of my journey helps you feel less alone, more seen, or a little braver... then it was worth every word.

Showing Up in the World

This journey has been deeply tied to my identity – and the growth that's come from sitting in the darkness. It's also been a whirlwind of intense, emotional, and transformative experiences. I've been forced to ask big questions: Who am I? What do I stand for? How do I show up in the world?

As I was drafting the end of this book, I attended the RCN Congress in Liverpool. This was a pivotal moment. I represented the Autism Consultant Nurse Network and Autism Oxford UK, stepping into a space that once felt like home but now felt different. I was no longer just "Nurse Kim" – I was a CEO, a leader, and a disruptor. The Congress reminded me of the power of collective voices, but it also surfaced a new tension: can I be both? Do I have to choose between clinical and entrepreneurial?

Kim on the SEN in TEN Podcast

The truth is, I don't want to choose. I want to blend. I want to lead with compassion and clinical insight. I want to build systems that work – not just for a few, but for everyone.

Alongside rebranding Autism Oxford UK's website, in 2025 I launched my own Kimberley Ashwin website. This was part branding, part declaration. But creating a website about yourself is tough. It feels egotistical. That imposter narrative pops up and whispers, "Why on earth would you have a website about you. Who do you think you are?" It's vulnerable work. But if you want to make a difference, people need to know you exist. You have to stretch yourself and move your ambitions forward.

The year when I descended into darkness taught me to be real, be authentic, and do what matters. The website (and this book) has been a declaration of who I am, what I believe in, and how I want to be seen. It lets me control the narrative instead of the narrative controlling me. The empowerment that comes with this cannot be underestimated. And seeing my story, our team, and our mission reflected online made it feel real. It was a moment of pride, but also deep vulnerability. Putting yourself out there – fully and unapologetically – is never easy.

All of this has brought my identity into sharper focus. I've felt the pull of old roles and the pressure of new ones. There are moments when I miss the clarity of clinical work – the protocols, the predictability. But I've also felt the excitement of building myself back from the foundations.

I've come to realise that identity isn't fixed. It's layered, evolving, and sometimes messy. I'm not just a nurse or a CEO. I'm a mother. A wife. A survivor. A strategist. A storyteller. And I'm learning to hold all those parts of me with pride.

Kim and Chris

Personal growth isn't a destination – it's an ongoing practice. It means pushing beyond your comfort zone, embracing new challenges, and always seeking opportunities to learn. For me, personal growth has meant confronting imposter syndrome, building confidence, and embracing my story.

Learning Point:
Becoming Yourself Is the Bravest Work You'll Ever Do

This journey has shown me that growth doesn't always look like success from the outside. Sometimes it looks like vulnerability, like hitting the publish button on a website that feels too personal, or standing in a room wondering if you belong. But it's in these moments that we build the deepest kind of strength.

Give yourself permission to evolve. To hold all parts of your story. To blend the old and new, and to lead with all of who you are.

Chapter 14
Just Getting Started

Reflecting on this journey, I am filled with a sense of pride and accomplishment. The growth of Autism Oxford UK is a testament to resilience, determination, and the power of a shared vision. Personally, this has been a transformative experience – pushing me to confront my insecurities and embrace leadership. Professionally, it's been deeply rewarding to witness the impact we're having in the autism community and beyond.

And I'm not done yet. I'm just getting started!

Looking ahead, my national contributions are far from over. I am excited for what the future holds and remain committed to breaking barriers and creating a more inclusive world for all. Whether through policy, practice, or advocacy, I remain committed to driving systemic change and innovation. My focus is clear: to create a world where neurodivergent individuals and their families don't just survive, but thrive.

This mission is personal. My own experiences have shaped it. My children continue to inspire it.

They've taught me about resilience, empathy, and unconditional love. I'm grateful that they have taught me to see the world differently, to fight for inclusion, and to model strength. Their journeys continue to inspire me every day, reminding me why I do what I do and fuelling my drive to create lasting change. One of my proudest moments was seeing my eldest follow his passion for sports photography – not influenced by others, but led by his own values. That moment affirmed everything I believe about giving our children the space and support to become who they are meant to be.

My ambition is to be the best mother I can be. To give my three children opportunities I never had. To create a home that's nurturing, supportive, and full of possibility. That means being present, listening, encouraging their dreams, and fighting for their rights. My children have been my greatest teachers, showing me what truly matters.

My ambition also lies in the continued growth of Autism Oxford UK – creating meaningful employment for neurodivergent individuals, building an inclusive workplace, where everyone feels supported and valued, and where their unique strengths are recognised and celebrated.

This means providing training and development opportunities, creating an inclusive work environment, and advocating for policies that support neurodivergent employees. I think often of one of our early colleagues – filled with anxiety and low confidence when she joined. With the right support and accommodations, she thrived in her role. Seeing her confidence grow and her sense of purpose develop was incredibly fulfilling, and she went on to write successful blogs about her journey. This reinforced my belief in inclusive workplaces and the impact of genuine support and opportunities for everyone to succeed.

I'd like to continue expanding our reach and impact. We aim to further reduce waiting times, enhance our post-diagnostic support services, and advocate for systemic changes that prioritise the needs of neurodivergent individuals and their families. I am committed to fostering a culture of continuous improvement and innovation within our organisation. By staying attuned to the evolving needs of our clients and embracing modern technologies and approaches, we can ensure that our services remain relevant and effective.

One of the lessons I have learned is the importance of collaboration. Creating systemic change requires working together with others who share your vision and values. This means building partnerships, collaborating with other organisations, and working together to advocate for change. It also means listening to the voices of those you are advocating for and ensuring that their perspectives and experiences are at the centre of your work.

Creating systemic change is not easy, and there will be challenges and setbacks along the way. However, it is important to stay focused on your mission and to keep pushing forward, even when things get tough. This means staying resilient, staying committed, and staying true to your values.

I will continue to stretch myself. I am committed to seeking out new learning opportunities, to embracing new challenges, and to pushing myself. I am also committed to using my experiences to inspire and to advocate for change. As I continue to make a difference, I am committed to staying true to my values and to the lessons I have learned along the way. This means leading with humility, prioritising the needs of others, and staying focused on my mission to create a more inclusive society.

My Invitation to You

Whatever your goal or mine, one thing I've learned is that we don't have to wait until we're "ready" to begin. We just have to start. So, wherever you are right now – start there.

And if you ever feel that people like you don't write books, lead organisations, or make a difference – know that they do. Because I did. And you can too.

I want to end this book with some final lessons I've taken from my journey, and I hope they will support you in yours:

1. **Resilience and Determination:** The ability to bounce back from setbacks and keep moving forward has been crucial. Whether facing personal challenges or professional obstacles, resilience has been the cornerstone of my journey.

2. **The Power of Support:** Surrounding myself with supportive individuals – from family to mentors – has made all the difference. The support network might not look traditional, but it will be there. You just need to find it.

3. **Embracing Vulnerability:** Being open about my struggles and seeking help when needed has been transformative. Vulnerability is not a weakness; it is a strength that allows for growth and connection.

4. **Continuous Learning:** This journey has been a constant learning experience. Embracing new opportunities, seeking knowledge, and being open to growth have been key to my success.

5. **Breaking Barriers:** Challenging the status quo and pushing for change has been a driving force. Whether advocating for neurodivergent individuals or redefining leadership, breaking barriers has been essential.

6. **Dreaming Big:** Don't be afraid to dream big and want more. Keep your dreams flexible and open to evolution. Not everyone will understand or agree with them – and that's OK. What matters is that you stay true to yourself.

Even When it Feels Hard, Keep Going – You Are Not Done Yet.

I believe in the power of story, in the possibility of change, and in the importance of dreaming big. Not everyone will understand your dreams. Some will dismiss them. But that's OK. Keep going anyway.

What's Next?

As part of sharing my story more widely, I've begun speaking publicly and appearing on podcasts to talk about my experiences, the lessons I've learned, and the ongoing work of Autism Oxford UK. It's been both empowering and humbling to connect with others in this way – turning my journey into something that can support and inspire change.

The growth of Autism Oxford UK is just the beginning. I will continue building my authentic self into someone stronger, more grounded, more compassionate – to myself and others.

While Autism Oxford UK will always be "my baby", my ambition reaches far beyond. I want this story to go far and wide, to reach the disadvantaged underdogs, and show them what's possible.

However Big the Dream, Start Where You Are – And Just Begin.

Connecting with me

I'm always open to connecting with those who share a passion for advocacy, leadership, and personal growth. If you're looking for a speaker, guest, or expert voice for your podcast or media piece, I'd love to hear from you.

Here's how you can get in touch:

- LinkedIn: Kimberley Ashwin

- Instagram: @kimberleyashwin

- Website: www.kimberleyashwin.co.uk

Thank you for joining me on this journey. The story is far from over, and I am just getting started. Together, we can continue to break barriers, create change, and build a more inclusive world for all.

About
Kimberley Ashwin

Kimberley Ashwin, RNLD, BSc, DipHE, is an Autism Consultant Nurse and the CEO of Autism Oxford UK. She is a proud mother of three uniquely wonderful children, two of whom are autistic, dyslexic, and have ADHD. As a SEN mum, Kimberley has firsthand experience navigating complex health and education systems to advocate for her children – an experience that fuels her passion for systemic change and inclusive practice.

A registered learning disability nurse with the Nursing and Midwifery Council (NMC), Kimberley developed her commitment to supporting autistic individuals early in her career. She has pursued advanced education in autism, learning disabilities, and co-occurring mental health needs, with a specialist focus on the autistic PDA profile and its overlap with ADHD. She is trained in a range of diagnostic tools and provides clinical leadership to a multidisciplinary team at Autism Oxford UK.

Kimberley has led the development of services across both the NHS and independent sectors. She co-chairs the National Autism Consultant Nurse Network, has served as an independent clinical advisor for Care (Education) and Treatment Reviews (C(E)TRs), and contributed to national guidance as a member of the NICE committee for ADHD.

Her leadership has been recognised through national awards and invitations to speak at conferences and policy forums. She has completed extensive leadership programmes and is known for her ability to bridge lived experience with clinical expertise.

Teen Mum to CEO is Kimberley's first book – a deeply personal and powerful account of overcoming adversity, healing from trauma, and building a life of purpose and independence. Through her story, she hopes to inspire others to believe in their worth, embrace their journey, and lead with compassion.

Acknowledgements

This book would not have been possible without the unwavering support of my husband, Chris, and my three beautiful children. Your love, patience, and encouragement have been my anchor throughout this journey. Thank you for believing in me and for being my constant source of inspiration.

My brother, for being my ultimate protector and sacrificing himself for me at the very beginning. None of this would have been possible without him.

I would also like to personally thank my one and only Nan – her stability and constant presence has taught me more than she will ever know.

I would also like to extend my heartfelt gratitude to my business mentor, James Martin from GainMore Solutions. Your guidance, wisdom, and encouragement have stretched my potential and pushed me to work outside of my comfort zone. Thank you for believing in my vision and for helping me navigate the complexities of the business world.

A special thank you to Liz Williams, previous boss, dear colleague and friend, who played a pivotal role in my professional development. Your mentorship and support have been invaluable, and your belief in my abilities has been a driving force in my journey.

To Sally Greenwell, the team manager of the community learning disability team, thank you for believing in my potential early in my career. Your encouragement and support have been instrumental in shaping my path.

To the incredible team at Autism Oxford UK, thank you for your dedication, hard work, and unwavering support. Your commitment to driving change and opening up support to the neurodivergent community is truly inspiring. Together, we have created a workplace that values diversity and inclusion, and I am grateful for each one of you.

I would also like to acknowledge the support of Claire Powell, Jo Dawson, and Lucy Barton, my team members who have been there through thick and thin and supported this book. Your support, collaboration, and friendship have made this journey all the more meaningful.

Lastly, I want to thank all the neurodivergent individuals and their families who have shared their stories and experiences with me. Your resilience, strength, and unique perspectives have been a source of inspiration and have fuelled my drive to create lasting change. This book is dedicated to you and to everyone who believes in the power of inclusion and diversity.

Thank you to everyone who has been a part of this journey. Your support, encouragement, and belief in my vision have made this book possible. Together, we can continue to drive change and create a more inclusive world for all.

List of Abbreviations

ADHD   attention deficit hyperactivity disorder

CQC   Care Quality Commission

DMT   disease-modifying treatments

GP   general practitioner (= primary care doctor in the UK)

MS   multiple sclerosis

NICE   National Institute for Health and Care Excellence

NHS   National Health Service

NMC   Nursing and Midwifery Council

PDA   pathological demand avoidance

PTSD   post-traumatic stress disorder

SEN   special educational needs

SENCO Special Educational Needs Coordinator

SpLD specific learning difficulties

9 781919 211909